A MINNESOTA CHRISTMAS
ANTHOLOGY

^a *Minnesota Christmas*

anthology

Edited by
Stephen E. Engels

Partridge Press
St. Cloud, Minnesota

Cover Art: Christmas Eve on the Flats by S. Chatwood Burton, 1919. From the collections of the Minnesota Historical Society. Used with permission. (See selection page 79.) Cover design by Ann Blattner.

Projects Editor, Theresa Rice Engels
Associate Editor, Vicki Lopez-Kaley
Book Design, Ann Blattner
Editor, Stephen E. Engels

ISBN 0-9621085-0-2
Copyright © 1988 Stephen E. Engels
Typography by North Star Press of St. Cloud, Inc.
Printed in the United States of America by Sentinel Printing, Inc.

Partridge Press
P. O. Box 364
St. Cloud, Minnesota, 56302
612-253-1145

Well, here we is, chilluns, and here it is Christmas. Now we all knows we's here cause it's Christmas, don't we? But what I want to know is who is going to tell me how come its Christmas?

Roark Bradford,
How Come Christmas

CONTENTS

KEEPING CHRISTMAS

CELEBRATING THE FEAST

CHRISTMAS IS COMING

A SENSE OF PLACE

CELEBRATING THE NATIVITY

CHRISTMAS RECIPES

ACTIVITIES

Newspaper accounts of Christmas in Minnesota: *The Minnesota Pioneer*, St. Paul; *The Daily Minnesotian*, St. Paul; *The St. Peter Herald*; *The Minnesota Democrat*, St. Paul; *The Minnesota Chronicle & Register*, St. Paul; *The Prison Mirror*, Stillwater; *The St. Cloud Journal*; *The St. Paul Pioneer Press Dispatch*; *Star Tribune*, Minneapolis; *Fairmont Daily Sentinel*

Getting Ready for Christmas
W. L. Sheppard, c. 1882

KEEPING CHRISTMAS

A Day of Praise and Thanksgiving

A Proclamation by Alexander Ramsey,
Governor of the Territory of Minnesota

"The Harvest is past, the Summer is Ended," the corn and the wheat that stood thick upon our fruitful soil, have been "gathered into the garner." Once more "cold out of the North" has come, "frost is given and the breath of the water is straightened." Before the year closes, it seems a becoming act for the people of Minnesota, by public assembly and solemn observance, to unite in giving thanks to Him "who crowneth the year with goodness," and whose blessings "are more in number than the sand."

In accordance, therefore, with a time-honored and now general custom of the states of the Republic, I respectfully recommend to the people of this territory the observance, in the way that is most appropriate, of Thursday, the 18th Day of December, as a day of Praise and Thanksgiving.

The Minnesota Pioneer, St. Paul, Minnesota
December 18, 1851

❧   ❧   ❧

Nothing could be cozier than our cabin Christmas eve. We had brought solid silver knives, forks and spoons. These hung from racks. Quantities of copper and brass utensils burnished until they were like mirrors hung in rows. In Sweden mother had woven curtains and bed coverings of red, white and blue linen and these were always used on holidays. How glad we were they were the national colors here! We covered a hoop with gay colored paper and set little wooden candle holders that my father had made all around it. This was suspended from the ceiling, all aglow with dips. Then, as a last touch to the decorations, we filled our brass candle sticks with real candles and set them in the windows as a greeting to those living across the lake. A sheaf for the birds and all was done.

Mrs. C. A. Smith, 1858

To-day is Christmas! Yes, the birth-day of our Saviour, Jesus Christ! That joyous, happy day

"Which to the cottage and the crown,
Brought tidings of salvation down."

And how do we observe it? Some by rioting and drunkenness; others by dining on roast turkey, plum pudding, and mince pies; but by far the greatest majority do not observe it at all, but go on with their ordinary evocations—buying, selling, etc., and some make it even a point of conscience to have extra household duties performed on this day, such as washing or cleaning house, for instance. And yet nearly all these people call themselves Christians! And nearly all of them keep up the Fourth of July, Washington's Birthday, etc. And very properly, too; it would be a disgrace if they did not. But how much more disgraceful and grossly inconsistent is it for an intelligent people professing themselves lovers and disciples of Christ, to pass by his birthday with so little reverence! Let us think of these things, my friends, and resolve for the future to keep up this day of all days in the year, as it ought to be kept. A day of joy and rejoicing, a day of praise and gratitude, a day of innocent mirth and merry-making—one that our children shall look back upon in all their after-wanderings as the pleasantest day of the whole year.

The Daily Minnesotian, St. Paul, Minnesota
December 25, 1857

Since today is the third Sunday in Advent, Christmas is drawing near and I may wish you a joyful Christmas and a good and happy New Year. These holidays, which are so much celebrated and so looked forward to by the young people in Sweden, are not much observed in America and are celebrated almost alone by Scandinavians and Germans. So if Christmas or New Year's Day comes on a weekday, you will see among the Americans that their shops are open the whole day and the miners and loggers go to work as usual, and the only change in their diet is a turkey and a drink of liquor. But what can you do about it? We eat wheat bread every day; pork, beef, chicken, eggs, butter, cheese, milk, and beer are everyday food. When we consider the old Swedish custom of living high, wide, and handsome for a few days, with fine bread, fish, and rice pudding, and then after two or three days going back to the usual coarse fare, that is just to play tricks on your stomach and appetite. The children here enjoy themselves as usual at Christmas, the youngest with a few small toys for Christmas presents and the older ones with snowballs and dances, sleigh rides, and so on.

Letters from the Promised Land, December 14, 1879

Christmas in a Sod House
by Hugo Nisbeth
translated by Roy W. Swanson

Nisbeth, a Swedish traveler, visited Minnesota in 1872 and 1873. Upon his return to Sweden he published a book entitled Two Years in America *from which the following account is taken. State historians believe the sod home described in the text was located near the town of Kandiyohi, east of Willmar, Minnesota.*

After about a four months' absence from Minnesota—during which time I traveled through Iowa, Nebraska, Illinois, and Wisconsin, and visited the larger cities on the eastern coast of North America, as well as crossed Canada in different directions—I returned to "the land of ten thousand lakes" in the middle of December, 1872. When last I was there waving fields of grain greeted my eye, and green pastures, and a happy, industrious people who joyfully turned to account the rich harvest with which the state had been blessed. Now all was changed. Winter had spread its white blanket over the fields, the trees had discarded their green dress and taken on their hoarfrost attire, sparkling in the sun. No more could the sailing clouds mirror themselves in the sky-blue waters; even the proud "father of waters," the mighty Mississippi, had been forced to let himself be imprisoned by the conquerer who now wielded the scepter. That the winters are severe here cannot be denied, and the winter of 1872 could reasonably be counted as one of the coldest in the memory of man. But the air here is thin and clear, and when one sees the blue smoke rising in coquettish rings from the log cabins at the edge of some huge pine forest, and at the same time sees the *bonde* out in the wood lot busy with the chopping, one thinks one is seeing again the fresh, charming picture that so often meets the eye of the traveler in our northland provinces in the winter. It is not the winter itself that the settler out on the thinly populated prairie looks forward to with dread, for the harvest has been garnered and sold, the larders are full, and the cattle have been lavishly supplied with fodder for the period during which they cannot go out. No, it is winter's companion, the terrible blizzard, that he fears. And, in truth, he has reason to. Death is the inevitable lot of him who is foolhardy enough to instruct himself to it. The blizzards here, as in other parts of America, are not to be compared with even the worst of our snowstorms at home, for they spring up more suddenly, and the howling storm, which with terrifying speed races across the endless plains, drives before it a whirling mass of fine snow particles that take away the breath, quickly cover up every track, and make it impossible to see even a distance of a few ells. He who permits himself to be surprised out on the prairies by such a storm is truly in a pitiable situation. The icy wind numbs his limbs, he loses the direction he should follow to reach his goal, and in despair he at last sinks down in the snow drifts either to die or to be found long after the blizzard has passed in a condition that would leave scant hope for his recovery. Happily these blizzards are not a daily occurrence, although they are unfortunately not infrequent. This fact and the care that the settlers soon learn to take make serious accidents very uncommon.

Much activity prevailed in St. Paul when I got there. The handsome stores were filled with newly arrived articles, which were tasteful and often rather costly, intended as gifts for the coming holidays. There was a brisk sale of Christmas trees in the markets, and those streets along which the retailers had their shops were crowded with conveyances belonging to near-by farmers who were in town to buy gifts or delicacies for the Christmas table. It is not only the Scandinavians who celebrate Christmas here in America in a true ancient northern fashion, but even the Americans themselves have in late years begun to give more and more attention to this festival of the children and have as nearly as possible taken our method of celebration as a pattern. For example, most of them use fir trees with candles, confections, and other decorations, and so far as the number and costliness of the presents are concerned they often display a liberality that would amaze us Swedes. These Christmas presents are given in various ways. In the public schools, especially for younger children, the school officials usually arrange a huge fir, which stands for about eight days. On this tree the children's parents and friends hang small presents, which are distributed by the school-teacher. In the home the presents are sent with a message if the giver is someone outside the family, or they are distributed by a dressed-up Christmas mummer, who here goes under the name of "Santa Claus." Still another custom exists, although it is not used so commonly perhaps as the first two. If there is reason to expect presents, a stocking is hung up at bedtime in some convenient and well-known place and in it in the morning will be found the expected presents. Not a trace of our traditional *lutfisk* and rice porridge is found. There is no special menu for Christmas Eve. On the other hand there are few American homes in which the customary turkey is not served on the following, or Christmas, day.

As I had planned to spend my Christmas Eve with some of my countrymen out on the prairie, I left St. Paul a few days before Christmas and went by the St. Paul and Pacific one hundred English miles northwest to the Litchfield station. Here, after some trouble, I was fortunate enough to secure a sled in which I set out over the prairie to the west. There was no road, of course. The level country which I entered first lay like an enormous white cloth spread out before my eyes, and the only guide I had for the direction I was to take was a small pocket compass and the blue smoke columns that here and there at a considerable distance arose from the log cabins. The way was not particularly difficult to traverse, for on the flat prairie the snow distributes itself comparatively evenly. But when, after twenty or thirty miles, I came out on the rolling prairie, I met with greater difficulties. In some places the snow had drifted in considerable quantities between the hillocks, and had it not been for the hardy horses and the extraordinary strong conveyances that they have in the West, I should have had extreme difficulty in making headway.

Toward nightfall on the day before Christmas Eve I perceived far off the smoke from a human habitation, which, from what I could make out at a distance, should be a sod house. I was soon there and found that this, in truth, was the case, although it was one of the very best kind. That is to say, in this case, the owner had only half dug himself into the ground. Three tiers of thick timbers were laid above ground and over these there was placed a roof with a slight pitch. One lived, so to speak, half under and half above the ground, and thus it became possible for the occupant to get daylight through a small window, which was sawed out of the south wall formed by the three timbers mentioned above. About twenty paces from the dwelling house was the granary and, annexed to it, the stable, also a half sod house, which was occupied by two oxen and a cow. Only a little grain was on hand; that which was not necessary for winter use had been sold, as usual, during Indian summer. The sod hay barn, on the other hand, seemed to be well filled with cattle fodder. I had not steered wrong, for I had reached the house of the man I sought, Jan Erikson from Wermland, who had been in America for three years and for the last two years had been living on his large eighty-acre homestead. I was received by him and his friendly wife with that cordiality which I have been accustomed to find among my countrymen on the prairie. Nor did I need to put forth any request that I might stay over Christmas Eve, for I was anticipated in this by my friendly hosts, who simply but heartily bade me remain and help myself to whatever they had to offer. To the two children, a girl of seven named Anna and a boy of three, Eric, the visit of a strange gentlemen seemed particularly surprising, but the sight of some packages I had brought along, which the dwelling's smallness made it impossible for me to hide, soon made us the best of friends.

Early in the morning of the day before Christmas my hosts were at work, and when I arose I found a huge ham already sputtering over the fire, while outside I heard my host's great ax blows, for he was busy getting the necessary Christmas wood ready. I hurried out and was met with a picture that was for me entirely new and particularly striking. The sun was about twenty degrees above the wavy horizon of snow and from the snow-clad tops of countless hillocks the sunbeams were thrown in a dazzling bewilderment all around. Yet, except for this tiny world in which I now found myself, I could not discern another sign of human presence than two columns of smoke, which arose, nearly perpendicularly, from the horizon, one in the northwest and one in the southwest. The first, explained my host, came from a sod house that was occupied the previous spring by the family of a German farmer who came from Illinois, where he had paid too much for his land and after two years of fruitless toil had been forced to leave everything with empty hands. In the other lived a Swedish family, a man and his wife and one child, who had lived there for a year and a half. After the wood was chopped and carried in, a task in which the two children took part with a will, the cattle were fed and watered, and a small sheaf of unthreshed wheat was set out for the few birds that at times circled around the house, in accordance with the lovely old Swedish custom.

With these and other chores the morning passed, and right after twelve o'clock we were invited in by the housewife for the midday meal. The cloth that covered the plain homemade table was certainly not one of the finest, but it was whole and clean, and the defects of arrangement that a fault-finding observer would have been able to point out were plentifully outweighed in my eyes by the unfeigned, cordial friendliness with which I was bade to help myself to what the house had to offer. For the rest, one should have felt ashamed not to be satisfied. The bread that we dipped in the kettle was freshly baked and tasty, and the fat chicken that was later served in a sort of stewed pie form, which awakened especially the children's delight, had clearly not fared ill during the short time allotted him to live. And so came the afternoon with its small arrangements for the evening meal and the Christmas table, for this could not be omitted. There was no Christmas tree, for fir trees are not yet planted in this part of Minnesota, but two candles stood on the white covered table and round these were placed a multitude of Christmas cakes in various shapes made by the housewife and such small presents as these pioneers were able to afford, to which I added those I had brought. Nor were *lutfisk* and rice porridge to be found on the table, but the ham which took the place of honor in their stead banished all doubt that the settler's labor and sacrifice had received its reward.

The meal was eaten in the happiest of moods and afterward the few presents were distributed to the children. The gifts were neither costly nor tasteful, but they were *gifts* and that was all that was necessary. On the wooden horse I had brought, the little three-year-old galloped over the hard-packed dirt floor of the sod house with as much joy and happiness undoubtedly as the pampered child upon one polished and upholstered. All was joy and thankfulness, and when later the head of the family read a chapter from the Bible about the Christ child I am certain that from the hearts of these poor people there rose many warm thanksgivings to Him who smoothed their path and gave them courage and strength to conquer the hardships of the New World.

Outside the snow fell slowly and spread its white Christmas mantle over the endless prairie. Now and then a snowflake fastened itself on the single window of the sod house, its curtains faded by the summer suns, and quickly dissolved and disappeared as if its icy heart had melted with joy at sight of the peace that reigned within. And later, from the corner of the room where the housewife's kind hands had made my bed, I heard the small voice of the youngest child, still clutching his wooden horse, repeating after his mother, "Good night, kind Jesus." Then it was I realized in full God's infinite wisdom when He willed to apportion "the palace for the rich, but joy for the poor."

Christmas Bread

Most immigrants to Minnesota seem to have had a recipe to dress up their everyday bread for Christmas. Stollen, Julekage, Pulla, Jolla Bread, or Vasilopita were made by substituting milk for water, adding eggs, sugar, dried fruits, nuts, and citron. It is in these additions and the type of flavoring preferred that the varying national traditions distinguish themselves.

To make 2 loaves of Christmas bread dissolve *2 pkg. dried yeast in ½ c. warm (not hot) water with 1 tsp. sugar;* mix and set aside about 10 minutes until the yeast has started. It will have a "yeasty" smell and be bubbly. Meanwhile, scald *2 c. milk* (cook over medium heat heat until bubbles form around edge—do not burn). Pour milk over *½ c. butter* in a large bowl and stir to cool and melt butter. Stir in *1 c. sugar* and *1 tsp. salt.* Cool to lukewarm, add *2 beaten eggs* then the yeast mixture.

Now it is time to decide on which addition of flavoring to make a distinctive traditional bread. The Scandinavians prefer cardamom; measure *1 tbsp. cardamom powder* or crush 8 whole seeds and add to liquid along with *1 c. finely chopped citron, 1 c. golden raisins, ½ c. currants* for Ule Kaga, Julekage or Icelandic Jolla Bread. The Finns might omit the fruit and would braid their cardamon bread in a fancy form as Pulla. Stollen, the German variation, keeps the dried fruit but omits the cardamom using *2 tbsp. brandy* as a flavoring along with *1 tsp. grated lemon rind,* and *1 c. finely chopped almonds.*

Now add *3 cups flour* and stir with a spoon to evenly mix ingredients, about 1 minute. Add *4-5 c. more flour,* until dough begins to leave the sides of the bowl. Turn out onto a floured board and knead about 10 minutes. Place bread in a greased bowl and cover with a wet cloth. Let dough rise until double in bulk in a warm spot, about 1 hour. Toss it onto a floured board and knead to remove air bubbles. Divide into 2 loaves and place in greased round 9″ pans or bread loaf pans. Cover and let rise again until doubled. Bake in a 350 degree oven for 40 minutes.

After removing from oven, brush tops with *melted butter and sprinkle with cinnamon and sugar,* or let cool and frost with a mixture of *1 c. powdered sugar, 1 tbsp. soft butter, 2 tbsp. milk, dash salt,* and *1 tsp. almond extract,* and decorate with *candied cherries or sliced almonds.* Or leave plain. Serve when cool or slice and toast. Freezes well after completely cooled.

TRE

The Brightest Memories

by Brenda Ueland

I see that Christmas evokes the brightest memories, so I will tell about it.

On the morning of Christmas Eve, the groceryman had brought the tree and Gus made a box for it. We had been stringing popcorn and cranberries for a day or two. And one of the most delightful things was sewing the candy bags out of yellow, red and green tarlatan. I loved doing this because it meant a most wonderful lordly state was to come, i.e., when we could each have a private candy bag and eat as much as we pleased. Think of it, between meals and continuously, walking around and blissful and looking on in contentment (just popping another piece in your mouth) at the holly on the banisters, the mistletoe in the chandelier, the *London Illustrated News* and *Sketch* and all the accumulated Christmas magazines of years, that Mother brought down from the attic.

And there were tremendous doings in the kitchen. You could go out and watch the interesting cleaning of chickens, scrape the cake bowl, and quietly eat long strips of raw cookie dough.

In the morning we trimmed the tree. The beauty and delight of Christmas tree ornaments! But everybody feels that. Mother brought down the boxes from the attic and we found all those nonpareil, exquisitely adorable, lovely baubles: the big, heavy, silver balls, the star for the top, a silver bird with tails of glass wire, a tiny bugle that really blew. Each child looked for his dearest and most precious trinket and put new thread on it and then hung it uneasily and stood back and surveyed it with utter love. And it was on this morning that the lordly candy-eating began.

We trimmed the tree. At noon it was all finished and white sheets were tacked down all over the library floor. Then Mother pulled out of the walls the large, sliding, paneled oak doors. The library was now sealed off from the rest of downstairs.

Christmas Eve we had a Norwegian supper. There was rolled spiced mutton, Christmas bread with citron in it, brown goat's milk cheese, a cheese in glass which smelled so frightful that only Father of all the grown-ups could taste it. Ludefisk. This is codfish treated in some way so that it has a queer smell that goes sailing through the house. The big people liked it, but the children always came to the table holding their noses: "Ick!" "Icky!" "Ish!" they cried.

"Please, dear, don't. It isn't polite."

But we kept it up all during the meal in a lower key, or by making faces. It was a great satisfaction to show repulsion for ludefisk, for we are always so terribly proud of our dislikes.

After supper the party began. More parents and children came, and mounds of overshoes, leggings and mittens on strings filled the window seats. At last the library doors were opened and there was the tree lit with candles. Then Mother distributed the presents among all the company. But most of our presents we got in the morning. Each child put a chair at the fireplace and pinned a long stout black stocking to the mantlepiece.

Christmas was bliss. But there came the time when it turned to gall, to the bitterest disappointment. When I was a small child, everything seemed so wonderful—those mechanical toys, the jack-in-the-boxes. But at nine or ten, suddenly all presents were just a frightful disappointment, such a blow, so peanutty and measly compared to what I had hoped for.

I began to want something like a diamond ring or a revolver. Instead I seemed to get such awful cheesy things. Once it was a celluloid lobster. My pain and shock at this were beyond description. I went upstairs and cried. Oh, dear, that was a terrible experience. "A pink celluloid lobster! But why? How could Mama? What a cheap, what a meaningless thing! How could she do that to me?"

Once at the Christmas Eve party I got a ring, a cluster of chipped turquoises shaped like a five-petal flower. I told myself, bracing up my expected agony (it was perhaps the second or third year of bitter Christmasses) that it was a good present, a pretty present. A real ring. "See, I got a ring. Isn't it pretty? Look, it's turquoise!" (though I wanted a diamond ring). But in almost no time I discovered that the gold came off black on my finger. The ring would have been all right, but it was not gold at all; that wire was homely, dark, cheap metal underneath. And later in the evening one of the microscopic blue petals fell out.

The next day it was bright winter and there was deep white snow as always. Diamonds sparkled on it. The high drifts along the driveway had thin eaves with dark caverns under them. We had Christmas dinner, turkey and all that, and then we went over to the woods to slide down hill.

"If only I had got a sled, that would be something like it," I thought. I had sleds enough, but they were just community-owned sleds that cluttered up the barn. They were the very low kind with pointed runners, fine for running with and hurling yourself down on your belly. "But say a flexible flyer. Why couldn't they give me that? Something new and bright and really worth something?"

The youngest Bruder boy came over into the woods and was sliding with us—Hector, an odd-looking blond child of six, in a ragged bundle of clothes.

"What did you get for Christmas, Hector?"

"Oh, some oranges," he said lightly.

Oranges! Oh, poor Hector. Oranges for Christmas! Imagine. There was worse than what happened to me by a million-scillion times. I felt terribly sorry for him, and for the first time I was able to see a little glimmer of philosophy about Christmas, about presents.

But take the Wetmore girls. They were certainly poorer than we were. We lived in a much bigger house anyway. I went to see them on Christmas Day, and there were their presents laid out on chairs. And so many things! Such a wonderful fancy complexity of presents: handkerchiefs, hair-receivers, baby pins, perfume bottles, a hundred things for each, with cards and names of givers attached and all sorts of fancy painstaking business: towels with initials embroidered on them! Now I certainly did not covet towels or hair-receivers or knitted booties for bed, but I envied the rich boodle, the sum of it, and the excitement and fuss about it.

You see Mother was characteristically sensible and wise. (Sigurd suffered the same way that I did; there was the year he got that acme of dullness, a map of the United States.) There were seven children, and it was hard work and expensive to have them all extravagantly pleased. So she bought a lot of things, and then, the night before Christmas, judiciously divided them fairly and sensibly among us all. Perhaps the map was taken from Sigurd's chair and put on Elsa's. "But no, I guess Elsa had better have the bird book and Sigurd the map." All very sensible.

But it made me many years later anxiously indulgent toward my own child. I cannot bear to have her ever disappointed, and at Christmas I get her five times too much and go into debt for two months. She must be absolutely surfeited. I tell you I cannot bear disappointment in anyone. It is a barbed spear that tears my soul. I cannot endure it. I cannot let them down.

The Cut-Glass Christmas
by Susan Allen Toth

The December after my father died, when I was seven and my sister was nine, we worried about Mother. We knew she was going to feel bad on Christmas Day, and we wanted to do something special but we didn't know what it could be. We huddled in the bathroom, whispered in corners, argued intensely in our bedroom after lights out and—unusual for us—at last came to an agreement. We would be Mother's Santa; we would fill a stocking for her just as she did for us. How surprised she'd be on Christmas morning to see her very own stocking hanging there on a drawer pull of the maple bureau in our living room! We felt sure that would cheer her up.

A week before Christmas we emptied our piggy banks and set out for Woolworth's, where we always bought our presents. Woolworth's was the Santa-Claus-and-Christmas-tree part of Christmas. It blazed with lights in the after-school dark, smelled of peanuts and popcorn at a counter heaped for the season with chocolate-covered cherries with cellophane-wrapped, red-and-white candy canes, rang with "Jingle Bells" and "Hark! the Herald" on a radio turned up loud near the cash register. Every year we each were allowed to pick out one new ornament from the tree-trimming counter, where we fondled brilliant glass balls, folding tissue-paper bells, and colored electric lights that bubbled when you plugged them in. No other store in our small Iowa town had the glitter and gleam that Woolworth's had at Christmas.

First we headed for our two traditional counters for Mother's presents—cosmetics and kitchen utensils. Although Mother never wore make-up, I wouldn't give up hope, encouraging her with a fake tortoise-shell compact of red rouge or a tiny bottle of Evening in Paris perfume or a set of mascara brushes. My sister was fond of small silver funnels, metal straining spoons, glass measuring cups. But this Christmas we felt none of our usual gifts would be quite right for a special stocking. We wandered up and down the rows, pondering pencil sharpeners, packaged stationery in floral cardboard boxes, little china dogs that were really salt and pepper shakers. We rejected a card of assorted needles from England, a fat red pincushion with an attached strawberry-shaped emery ball, an earring tree. The tree was gold-colored metal and spun on a plastic base, but unfortunately, our mother did not wear earrings.

At last we found ourselves together, discouraged, at a back counter, hidden behind toys and semidarkened under a burned-out fluorescent light, where Woolworth's kept its glasses, dishes, pots and pans. We knew we couldn't affort a teakettle or a frying pan. Mother used empty jam jars for glasses and she didn't need any more silverware. But suddenly we both saw at the far end of the counter a section of cut-glass dishes—not just plain round cereal bowls, but jagged and deeply carved, dark-green glass. Small bowls were ten cents; a size big enough for soup or oatmeal was 20. I hurried to the end of the counter, where it was brighter. How the glass shone! My sister agreed that the fancy dishes were unlike anything Mother had. With our allowances pooled, we could buy six small bowls and two big ones. The clerk at the front packed the dishes carefully in newspaper and warned us to unpack them gently. The edges were sharp, she said. We hurried home in the dark, happy and warm inside with our secret. Eight cut-glass bowls! Mother would never have had such a Christmas!

On Christmas Eve my sister and I faced our only other problem—what to use for Mother's stocking. We each had a red felt Christmas stocking, hung year after year, but we hadn't had enough money to buy one for Mother. While she was washing dishes after supper, we tiptoed down the hall to her room and began to rummage through her dresser drawers. Winters were cold in Iowa, and Mother had several pairs of sensible cotton and wool anklets, but none of them seemed big enough. We could barely fit one small bowl into each sock. My sister lifted out a cardboard packet. "What about these?" she said. We looked at each other, then at the beige nylon stockings, never worn, folded neatly around the cardboard.

Mother didn't have many nylons; this was just a few years after the war and they were still expensive. But we knew these stockings would be big enough to hold our dishes. "I think if we're careful, it'll be okay," I said. We tiptoed out of the bedroom with the nylons hidden under my sister's skirt.

Early Christmas morning we crept quietly out of our beds, scarcely breathing as we passed Mother's door, desperately hoping she wouldn't hear our feet on the creaky wooden stairs. In the living room we hurriedly stuffed her stockings, using both nylons, yanking them wide to accommodate the jagged edges of the cut-glass bowls. We didn't try to hang them up. They were too heavy. Instead we propped them against the bureau that we used for Santa in the absence of a fireplace. Then we looked at the bulging stockings, grinned with pleasure at each other and ran to call Mother.

When she sleepily entered the living room, her eyes were immediately riveted to the bureau. Two green cut-glass bowls hung precariously over the tops of her stretched, snagged, new nylon stockings. "My!" she said "Did you girls do all this?" There was something odd in her tone, but she quickly recovered. "What absolutely beautiful bowls!" she said admiringly, sitting down on the floor and taking them out one by one, setting them in a row on the floor for us all to enjoy. She hugged us both. We were so proud we had pleased her. "You are wonderful girls to have thought of this, and I love you both very much," she said. She ignored the empty stockings on the floor beside her.

Now a mother myself, living alone with a nine-year-old daughter, at Christmas I think of many things, but always I remember that Christmas of the cut-glass bowls. To me it shines as a beacon my mother has left me, a beacon to guide me through the maze of conflicting feelings, emotional demands, free-floating guilt and worry that afflict me at this time of year. When my mother looked at those ruined stockings and ugly cut-glass bowls, which eventually disappeared into the deep recesses of her bottom shelves, she knew what Christmas was all about. "I love you both very much."

It is often hard for me to remember what Christmas is all about. As a teacher on the semester plan, I always find myself buried under term papers and final examinations just before Christmas, a weight that may not be lifted until New Year's, when grades are irrevocably due. Meanwhile a mountain of mail begins to build up on my dining-room table, from aunts, cousins, dear old friends, all of whom need to hear from me. I have presents to wrap hurriedly at the last minute.

My daughter has a sudden desperate desire to make things. The tree has to be planted firmly in its stand, lighted, decorated; where are the candles that always go on the mantle? Marking a paper with red pencil, trying to stay within the margins and be helpful but not unkind, I throw it down on the floor when the phone rings. Can we come to Sunday brunch across town? Will I bring a salad? I have no time at Christmas, no time at all.

So I try to think of the cut-glass bowls. I put Christmas carols on the hi-fi ("Play 'Rudolph, the Red-Nosed Reindeer' again, Mommy") and sit down to examine my own priorities. What do I want out of Christmas? What does it mean to me at the heart of the rustling tissue paper, blinking lights, ringing telephone? What must I find time to do? As I listen to the familiar carols my mind begins to clear. I realize first that Christmas means, oddly enough, silence. At Christmas I feel more than ever a need to get away from myself, from others, and listen to the quiet. I find myself taking long walks after dark, walking by my neighbors' houses, looking at their trees blazing in the windows, admiring the cheerful displays on their outdoor evergreens. I listen to the crackle of frosty branches in the wind, the crunch of my footsteps on the ice, my own moist breath as I puff into a wool scarf that holds a faint scent of mothballs.

On a cold, bright night when the stars are out above the city and the remaining elms on our street cast strange, dark patterns on the white snow, it seems to me while I walk that I can listen to time passing. I can almost hear the year slipping by. I always feel a little sad, recalling past losses and failures, but then I think of what we celebrate at Christmas, a birth and a new beginning, and I am comforted. I can feel hope in the air and see it sparkle in the lighted trees. I have another chance. Next year maybe I will do better.

Sometimes during Christmas week, I promise myself, I will find a small family church where I can listen to the simple words of the King James version of the Nativity, with their promise and joy. I will see a straw creche, sing "Silent Night" and "It Came Upon the Midnight Clear," light a small candle myself and hold it briefly aloft, a token of continuing faith that somehow, somewhere, all will be well.

Walking down my street at night, I let my mind wander over the past. There I always meet old friends and invent conversations with them, trying to imagine what they look like now, asking them how they're doing. That is why I use Christmas as a time to restore damaged or dying relationships. During the holidays I recklessly run up my phone bill to call distant friends I'm worried about. What is Joyce doing in Richmond? Is Sally lonely this Christmas in London? Why haven't I heard from Linda in Vancouver? Has Larry recovered from his mother's death? I once startled an old lover by calling him after four years at Christmas to ask how he was, how the children were, did they visit often, was he happy. That call laid an unhappy ghost finally and completely to rest.

Then for weeks during January I answer my cards, glue snapshots of my daughter on top of printed messages, write short letters, ask a few questions that may not be answered until next Christmas, when the cards come again. One year my favorite Christmas card read simply, "Of all things this coming year, be careful of love." At Christmas I try to keep the small flames glowing on candles that may be burning out for want of care.

Perhaps as part of my wish to reaffirm bonds at Christmas, I also make some time to spend in my kitchen, baking special treats to share with others. I study glossy pictures in magazines, clip recipes, read them to myself at night in bed. If I didn't have a full-time job, I fantasize, I could spend the whole month creating gingerbread houses, turning out dozens of decorated cookies, rushing from door to door with loaves of swirled, candied, beraisined bread. As it is, I usually have to settle for one long Saturday morning surrounded by spotted, yellowing recipes never used; cake flour that seems a suspicious antique gray; fancy molds dug out from cobwebbed corners. Last year it was plum pudding, from scratch, with as many jeweled fruits as I could stuff into the batter—three plum puddings, actually, since my molds all were rather small. We ate one Christmas Day, gave one to friends to take home, shared another with neighbors later in the week. For days after the actual baking smells were gone, an aroma of warmth and sweetness seemed to linger in my kitchen.

I am always tired after Christmas. Sometimes I get cranky, catch cold, come down with a headache—signs of stress, I do not need to be told. It may be foolish to try to cram so much into an already bursting schedule, to sandwich concerts around exams to be graded, plum pudding between cards to be answered, a long walk under starlight when presents are waiting to be wrapped. But I cannot bring myself to give up any more of Christmas than I am absolutely forced to. I fervently pack it all in as my sister and I stuffed those glass dishes into Mother's stretching nylons so many Christmases ago. Like my mother, I want to set out the tokens of love on the living-room floor, look past their gaudy color and cut-glass gleam, ignore the ruined stockings that held them and remember why they are there.

Susan Allen Toth
Susan Allen Toth is the author of several books of recollections: "Blooming,"
"Ivy Days," and "How to Prepare for Your High-School Reunion." She
is currently professor of English at Macalester College in St. Paul.

A Child's Christmas in Lake Wobegon
by Garrison Keillor

Dad's fear was that Christmas would throw him into the poor-house. Mother felt that each of us should get one big present every year in addition to the socks, Rook game, paddleball set, model, ocarina, shirt, miscellaneous gifts: one *big* one, like a printing press or a trike or Lincoln logs. Dad thought the ocarina should be enough for anybody. He for one had never been given a toy as a child but *made* his own toys, as everyone did then, out of blocks of wood and string and whatnot, and was content with them, so the thought that a boy *needed* a large tin garage with gas pumps out front and crank-operated elevator to take the cars up to the parking deck was ridiculous to him and showed lack of imagination. "I don't want to know," he said when Mother walked in with a shopping bag full, but then he had a look, and one look made him miserable. "Twelve dollars? *Twelve dollars?*" He believed that spending was a tendency that easily got out of hand, that only his regular dis-approval kept Mother from buying out the store. It all began with Roosevelt who plunged the country into debt and now thrift was out the window and it was "Live for today and forget about tomor-row" with people spending money they didn't have for junk they could do without and Christmas was a symptom of it. He went into The Mercantile to buy a pair of work socks and saw a German music box that made him wonder what the world was coming to. Eight dollars for a piece of junk that played "Silent Night," which was maybe worth seventy-five cents, but there was Florian Krebsbach buying the thing who owed money to a list of people as long as your arm. That was Christmas for you.

The twin perils of the poorhouse and the exploding tree made for a vivid Christmas. Where the poorhouse was, I didn't know, but I imagined it as a gray stone house with cold dank walls where people were sent as punishment for having too much fun. People who spent twenty dollars here and twelve dollars there, thinking there was more where that came from, suddenly had to face facts and go to the house and stay in it and be poor. I might go with Dad or I might be farmed out to relatives, if the relatives wanted me, which probably they wouldn't, so I'd live in a little cell at the poor-house and think about all the times I had begged for Dad to buy me things. I would eat rutabagas and raw potatoes and have no toys at all, like Little Benny in *The Mysterious Gentleman; or, The Christmas Gruel; A True Story of an Orphan in the East London Slums,* except that Little Benny was patient and never complained or asked anything for himself and was adopted by a kind benefactor and brought into a life of fabulous wealth and luxury in a Belgravia mansion, whereas I, a demanding and rebellious and ungrateful child, was heading in the opposite direction, toward the dim filthy room and the miserable pile of rags for a bed and the racking coughs of our poor parents, dying of consumption from hard labor to earn money to buy the junk I demanded.

On the other hand, the danger of Christmas-tree fire some night killing us all in our beds seemed to point toward a live-for-today philosophy, not that we necessarily should go whole-hog and buy everything in the Monkey Ward catalog, but certainly we could run up a *few* bills, knowing that any morning could find us lying in smoldering ruins, our blackened little bodies like burnt bacon that firemen would remove in small plastic bags. Simple justice demands that a person who dies suddenly, tragically, at a tender age, should have had some fun immediately prior to the catastrophe. If your mother yells at you and you go off on your bike feeling miserable and are crushed by a dump truck—that would be a much worse tragedy than if it had been your birthday and you had gotten nice presents, including the bike, and were killed in a good mood.

Then one Christmas I opened a long red package and found a chemistry set, exactly what I wanted, and sat and stared at it, afraid to look inside. For Mother to buy me one, given her feelings, was more than adventurous, it was sheer recklessness on her part, like a gift of Pall Malls and a bottle of whiskey. The year before, I tried to aim her toward the Wards deluxe woodburning kit, pointing out that I could earn money by making handsome Scripture plaques, but she said it was too dangerous. "You'll burn down the house with it," she said. So, a year later, to get a chemistry set, complete with Bunsen burner, fuel, a little jar marked "Sulphur," and who knew what else, I didn't dare show how happy I was. "Thank you," I said, humbly, and put it aside and tried to look interested in what other people were getting, afraid that if I got too excited about chemistry, she'd want to have a closer look at it.

After a little elaborate politeness, thanking her for the nice socks and wonderful underwear, admiring my sister's dollhouse, I slipped away to the basement and set up my laboratory on a card table next to the laundry tubs. The instruction book told how to make soap and other useful things I didn't need, and omitted things I was interested in, such as gunpowder and aphrodisiacs, so I was on my own. I poured some liquid into a peanut butter jar and dumped some white powder in it—it bubbled. I poured a little bit on the table as an experiment and it hissed and ate a hole in the leather, which made me think, if it had spilled on me it would have eaten my hands off down to the wrists. Would it eat the jar? Would it eat the drain pipe? Had the makers of Junior Scientist included chemicals so deadly they might destroy a house? Upstairs everybody was enjoying Parcheesi, unaware of the danger. I got out a tube of thin metal strips that I thought must be solder, and lit a match to melt some onto a plastic cowboy to give him a coat of armor, but instead the strip burst into fierce white flame as bright as the sun—I dropped it on the floor and stomped it to bits. My cowboy's face was gone, his head a blackened blob drooped down on his chest—what I would look like if I kept fooling around. I packed away the chemistry set and stuck it on the shelf behind the pickled beets. Eight dollars wasted. My poor father. Little Benny sold matches on the streets of London in bitter weather to buy medicine for his sick father, but I was a boy who played with fire and came close to killing everybody. Poor me, too. My big present was a big joke. What was Mother thinking of?

I went upstairs and moped around in the doorway so they could see me, but they were too busy having a good time. I went up to my room to mope around up there, maybe someone would come and find me and ask what was wrong, but time passed and nobody did. Mother called up the stairs to ask if I was hungry, but when I yelled that I wasn't she didn't come to find out why. I went to the stairs to yell down that maybe I'd just go to bed, and as I was about to yell, I looked in the door to my sister's room and saw the dollhouse.

It was a two-story white house, two bedrooms upstairs, living room, dining room, and kitchen. I had helped her carry it to her bedroom and set it on the floor by her bed and arrange the furniture, and now the Peabodys were about to enjoy their Christmas dinner. Upstairs, their plastic beds were permanently made; downstairs, a perpetual fire glowed in the fireplace, their two tabby cats curled up on the floor.

Minutes later, the big olive-drab B-17 revved up its engines and roared off the flight deck and down the dark hallway. The poor helpless family, Phoebe and Pete Peabody and little Petey and Eloise, sat in their elegant dining room, their movable arms placed politely on the table, their smiling little faces turned toward the turkey, as the hum of the deadly aircraft came closer and closer. Their great protector was miles away, engrossed in Parcheesi. They sat in pathetic dignity as the craft circled overhead and finally came in on its bombing run, dropping tons of deadly Lincoln logs. Pete was the last to die, sitting at the head of the table, a true hero, and then it was all over and Christmas lay in ruins with clouds of smoke rising from it, and the bomber returned to the carrier, its crew jabbering and laughing in Japanese. But little Petey wasn't dead! He rose painfully from under a pile of furniture and limped out of the house. He was badly injured and would have to spend some time in a hospital until his burns healed, but somehow he would get over his frightful loss and grow up and be a normal, happy person.

In addition to having hosted the weekly radio show, "A Prairie Home Companion," Garrison Keillor has also written three national bestsellers, Happy to Be Here, Lake Wobegon Days, *and* Leaving Home. *He is a frequent contributor to the* New Yorker *magazine. He began his radio career at the University of Minnesota with station KUOM.*

Waiting for Christmas Day

by Harrison Salisbury

It was these Russian Jewish refugees from the autocratic rule of the czar who first began to open a bit wider the narrow doors of my Victorian world. They lived in a milieu of ideas, of culture, of philosophy, of literature, of mores which I did not know existed. They did not eat their meals at regular hours. They did not get up from the table after eating and go to a living room. They sat right at the kitchen table where they ate and talked and talked and talked. I never heard the end of an argument or the conclusion of a discussion. I always had to go home while it was still in progress (but this seemed to make little difference because the same argument would be going on the next day). Nor was there anything authoritarian about these arguments. Everyone took part and my opinion (if I had one)seemed to count as much as that of anyone else. It was a window on a different world and sometimes I was shocked by it, unexpectedly, when, for example, I asked the question of a Child of Plenty to a youngster across the street: "What are you having for Christmas dinner?" And she complacently replied, "Cheese sandwiches."

Cheese sandwiches for Christmas. Well . . . Christmas was the event of the year for me. I don't know how old my sister and I were before we broke the custom of getting into one or the other's bed trying to keep ourselves awake all night long on Christmas Eve, telling endless stories and waiting for the noises of the adults behind the closed door of the bedroom finally to cease so that we might silently slip out, hand in hand, through the mysterious heavy-scented darkness, through the dining room with its dimly gleaming silver and porcelain, through the living room where stockings hung bulging at the fireplace, and into the parlor—now a place of strange shapes and imponderable riddles, a Christmas tree silhouetted against the bay window, the scent of spruce mixed somehow with other fragrances—then tiptoeing back to bed, promising each other not to take another peek until the loud-ticking cuckoo clock struck three; probably sinking back into sleep and not awakening again until—horrors!—six o'clock, time to tumble into our parents' bedroom and wheedle them into staggering up, heavy-lidded, to set the fires going in the fireplaces, to shake up the furnace so that hot air began to billow up through the open registers and then, but only then, in heavy woolen bathrobes and fleece-lined bedroom slippers, to begin the ritual of the presents.

Yes, Christmas was *the* day of my childhood—a private day, really. Just the family. My aunt and uncle and cousin. Sometimes another aunt and uncle and cousin—if they were in Minneapolis. A day of excitement, of joy. Usually either my sister or I got sick. Sometimes both.

For weeks we had been building up to it. The anticipation started immediately after my birthday in mid-November. There were not-too-subtle warnings that Santa Claus was observing the conduct of young children with special care. And if one wanted his full attention and kind response, one had best give him no cause for displeasure—that is, eat your meals quietly and leave nothing on the plate, no joking or playing at the table; go to bed swiftly at the appointed hour, no "five minutes more"; do your chores without being told; pick up your boots, don't leave them strewn about the kitchen; see that your toys are in their places in the cupboard or the window seat, and don't leave the building blocks scattered around; and don't complain about errands to the basement and the woodshed.

Well, there were many more admonitions and they changed a bit, year by year, but that was the start of Christmas. Then came the composition of the letter to Santa Claus, a serious occupation which required much thought. One should not ask for too much—that would certainly cause him to think he was dealing with a greedy child. But, on the other hand, one should try to remember to put on the list the things one really wanted—otherwise how could he know what presents were the most essential? The list was usually completed just after Thanksgiving Day. Then the pace began to quicken. There were visits downtown, perhaps to Donaldson's Glass Block, the nearest thing to Brighton which Minneapolis boasted. A sight of Santa Claus with his bell and his chimney (soliciting alms for the Salvation Army or the Volunteers of America). Sometimes—heavens—two Santa Clauses were spotted and that required a bit of explanation. But the climax of the pre-Christmas activity was the visit to Holtzermann's store. I don't know how I managed to square this most wonderful of institutions with my deep-seated germanophobia. Holtzermann's was the most German of German stores. It had been transported direct from the Black Forest. It was crammed from top to bottom with German toys (and there *were* no other toys in the years coming up to World War I). Somehow, possibly through Captain von Boy-Ed and his U-boat, or more likely by prudent advance buying, the stock of German toys, the mechanized animals, the Anchor blocks, the miniature trees, the small chimes which played "Stille Nacht," the lebkuchen, the pfeffernusse, the gilded angels, the shepherds, the golden stars, and the crimson ornaments with German Christmas mottoes on them did not vanish in 1914. They went on through 1915 and 1916. Only in 1917 did Holtzermann's become more of a ghost than a store, with Japanese trinkets replacing the Black Forest music boxes and cuckoo clocks, but, miracle of miracles, the great basement bins of Dutch wooden shoes were somehow still filled to the brim. But no tin soldiers, no Prussian horsemen with their lances, no small leaden cannons, no banners and flags of grenadier regiments, no flaxen-haired dolls with slow-closing blue eyes, no stuffed animals with genuine leather hides. I did not cry on that wartime visit to Holtzermann's. I was too big a boy. But I felt like it. It was a dream vanished. A world that was never to return.

Nationally known journalist Harrison Salisbury has spent most of his career with the New York Times. *He is recipient of the Pulitzer Prize and author of numerous books. A native of Minnesota, his most recent work is* A Time of Change.

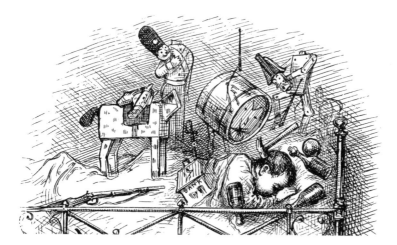

"There are many things from which I might have derived good by which I have not profited, I dare say," returned the nephew, "Christmas among the rest. But I am sure I have always thought of Christmas-time, when it has come round—apart from the veneration due to its sacred name and origin, if anything belonging to it can be apart from that—as a good time; a kind, forgiving, charitable, pleasant time; the only time I know of, in the long calendar of the year, when men and women seem by one consent to open their shut-up hearts freely, and to think of people below them as if they really were fellow-passengers to the grave, and not another race of creatures bound on other journeys. And therefore, uncle, though it has never put a scrap of gold or silver in my pocket, I believe that it *has* done me good, and *will* do me good; and I say, God bless it!"

Charles Dickens, *A Christmas Carol*

"Christmas," wrote Dickens, "is the only holiday of the year that brings the whole human family into common communion." We are scattered in many lands, yet the bond of union that has long held us together seems to strengthen with years. Many Christmas anniversaries have come and gone since we first assembled, in spirit if not in presence, to hang the holly and pledge our faith and friendship; and each recurring Christmas time has found us more closely united. Let us hope and believe that when even the toddlers of our family shall have seen their heads grow gray the spirit of Christmas shall still make young their hearts.

St. Peter Herald, St. Peter, Minnesota
December 31, 1886

Hurrah for the Pudding!
From *Little Folks*, c. 1870

CELEBRATING
THE FEAST

German Table Prayer

Komm Herr Jesus	Come Lord Jesus
sei unser gast	Be our Guest
und segne	And let
Was Du uns	Thy Gifts to us
bescheret hast.	be blest.
Amen.	Amen.

Extensive preparations are being made for the celebration by religious observance and social festivities. It is wisdom to enjoy and not abuse the good things in life. May all our friends enjoy a truly happy Christmas.

Minnesota Democrat, St. Paul, Minnesota
December 24, 1850

Christmas will be with us next Tuesday, and every one is preparing to enjoy it as seemeth best to suit them. The grave and devout will be at church. Those that love worldly pleasure will be at the several balls, or out upon sleighing, and eating and drinking parties. The great centre of attraction for this class is the ball at the "Minnesota House," Stillwater, on Christmas night, on which occasion "mine host," Hartshorn, expects to "lay himself out," and surpass every thing of the kind yet got up in the Territory.

Minnesota Chronicle and Register, St. Paul, Minnesota
December 22, 1849

29

We had a very pleasant service Christmas, went to service and Mr. and Mrs. Peake (The Episcopal Clergyman at Crow Wing) came home to dinner with us and we enjoyed our oyster soup, roast turkey, and plum pudding, coffee and fixings largely. . . . After dinner, we all went down to the Fort [Fort Ripley] and spent a pleasant evening. The Christmas tree looked beautiful. I found a very pretty embroidered cushion for me and Sam came into possession of a watchcase with a mouse on it, with other funny things. . . .

Well, besides our evening at the Fort, Mr. Boileau gave a party Thursday evening, at his house. Sent to St. Cloud for music (eighty miles) had an elegant supper and though not as elegant as some of our St. Paul affairs of the kind, wasn't to be despised.

Elizabeth Kingsley Fuller, 1853

Oyster Stew

Oysters were a mainstay of the Christmas menu for those of Yankee and Scotch-Irish backgrounds and embraced by new arrivals of other nationalities as well. Barrels of oysters packed in ice made the trip west for the Christmas holidays even on the frontier; the advent of the canning process in the 19th century made them a treat available to all.

This fish soup needs very little heat and indeed, overcooking toughens the oyster and threatens to curdle the cream. Cooked in the top of a double boiler over, not in, hot water, this recipe is nearly foolproof. First, sauté *1 tsp. grated onion* and *a sliver of garlic* in *2-4 tbsp. butter* and remove from heat. Transfer to top of a double boiler and add *1 to 1½ pints oysters with liquid, 1½ c. milk, ½ c. cream (or ½ and ½), ½ tsp. salt, 1 tsp. paprika, 1 tsp. Worcestershire sauce,* and *⅛ tsp. white pepper.* Cook over, not in, boiling water. When milk is hot and oysters float, serve at once.

TRE

Red Rock Christmas Plum Pudding
by Marjorie M. Engels

The following recipe was given to my mother in 1915 but no doubt is much older and has been handed down over a long period of time. The neighbor and friend from whom it came was an elderly English-Scotch immigrant whose husband, "Bach" did some work for my family. They lived a block from our house in a large Victorian home, an intriguing place for us children to visit. At times Mrs. Bachelar allowed us to visit the bedrooms of their home. Each one was done in a different color. The rose room had been their daughter's and the blue room their son's. They seemed cold and empty to us as youngsters because they were vacant. Sometimes we were allowed to play the pump organ. That was a great pleasure because we only had a piano at our home. Mrs. Bachelar kept a bird that sang. After a visit we were often sent off to gather seeds from a certain weed and bring them back to the bird. The other day as I walked along the path at William O'Brien State Park, I was tempted to pull a few weeds for whose bird I don't know.

The Bachelars enriched our lives as children growing up in a small settlement then known as "Red Rock" and now incorporated into the village of Newport, Minnesota.

Recipe of Mrs. A. Bachelar, 1915

The "plums" involved aren't plums at all or even prunes, but apples, raisins and currants. This recipe uses suet as a fat, instead of shortening or butter. A traditional ingredient seldom used today, suet melts gradually during the steaming process.

In a large bowl combine *2 c. finely chopped suet, 2 c. seedless raisins, 1 c. chopped apple, 1 c. currants,* and *1 c. light molasses* with *1 c. cold water.* Mix well and set aside. In a separate bowl combine *3 c. sifted flour, 1 tsp. soda, ½ tsp. salt, 2 tbsp. cinnamon, ½ tsp. cloves* and *½ tsp. allspice.* Add the dry ingredients to the first mixture and mix well. Fill well-greased pudding molds, or cans with tightly fitting lids like 1 lb. coffee cans, only 2/3 full. Place molds on a trivet in a heavy kettle over, not in, 1 inch simmering water. Cover kettle tightly and steam for 3 hours. Check water occasionally to make sure it hasn't boiled away. Remove from heat and take off lids of molds so that excess steam may escape. Let stand ½ hour and unmold.

Serve the pudding with the following sauce. Cream together *2 teacups sugar* and *2 teacups butter*. Add to this mixture *2 well-beaten large eggs* mixed with *1 teacup of red wine*. Stir and set on top of tea kettle or over boiling water. Never heat directly on top of stove or even allow pan to touch boiling water. Plum pudding is brought flaming to the table with a sprig of holly. To accomplish this heat *½ c. brandy*, pour over the pudding and light with a match.

Of Turkey, Wild Rice, and Cranberries

Fête de l'An

The last of December, 1679, on the banks of the river, we killed only a buffalo and some wild turkeys, because the Indians had set fire to the dry grass of the prairies along our route. The deer had fled; and in spite of the effort made to find game, we subsisted merely through the providence of God, who grants aid at one time that he withholds at another. By the greatest good fortune in the world, when we had nothing more to eat we found a huge buffalo mired at the river's edge. It was so big that twelve of our men using a cable had difficulty in drawing it onto firm ground.

After spending the day rejoicing, dancing, and feasting, we assembled the chiefs of the villages on either side of the river. We let them know through our interpreter that we Franciscans had not come to them to gather beavers, but to bring them knowledge of the great Master of Life and to instruct their children. We told them that we had left our country beyond the sea (or, as the Indians call it, the great lake) to come live with them and be their good friends. We heard a succession of loud voices saying "Tepatoui Nicka," which means "That is a good thing to do, my brother; you did well to have such a thought."

Father Louis Hennepin, 1680

Turkey and Wild Rice

On the first of November I arrived at Lake Pepin, a wide part of the Mississippi River. Great numbers of water fowl are seen on this lake and on the adjacent rivers: cranes, swans, geese, brants and ducks. In nearby groves are many turkeys and partridges. On the plains are the largest buffaloes of any in America.

Jonathan Carver, 1766

The land along the Minnesota River is excellent, with some good timber. The woods and prairies are full of animals: turkeys, buffalo, deer, caribou, elk and moose. Raccoons are very large. Snakes are small and not poisonous. Wolves are plentiful. They follow the buffalo and often kill the young and old.

Peter Pond, 1773

We eat a kind of rice, much like oats. It grows wild in the water three or four feet deep. This is their food for most of the winter. For each man they put a handful in the pot, and it swells enough to suffice. By this bounty we see that there is a God that shows himself in every country, who is almighty, full of goodness, the preservation of those poor people who know him not.

Pierre Esprit Radisson, 1659

On the right-hand side, eight leagues above the Falls of St. Anthony of Padua, is the narrow mouth of the Issati or Nadouessioux River [Rum River]. Ascending this river northward for about seventy leagues, one reaches Lake Buade or Issati, its source [Lake Mille Lacs]. We named the river St. Francis.

The lake spreads over vast swamps where wild rice grows. Wild rice is also found in many other places as far as the end of Green

Bay. This kind of grain grows in swampy land without being sown. It resembles oats but tastes better and has longer stems and stalks. The Indians gather it in season, the women binding many stalks together with basswood bark to prevent its being entirely eaten by the flocks of duck and teal found in the region. The Indians lay in a store of it for part of the year, to eat when their hunting season is over.

Father Louis Hennepin, 1680

Twenty miles above the mouth of the River St. Croix is the River St. Pierre, called by the natives Waddapawmenesotor [Minnesota River]. It falls into the Mississippi from the west. This is a fair, large river that flows through the country of the Sioux, a most delightful country. Wild rice grows here in abundance. At a little distance from the river are hills from which you have beautiful views. Near a branch of this river, called Marble River [in what is now Pipestone County, Minnesota], is a mountain from which the Indians get a sort of red stone, out of which they hew the bowls of their pipes. This country also abounds in a blue clay that serves the Indians for paint. Blue is regarded as a mark of peace, as it resembles the blue of the sky, a symbol of peace.

Jonathan Carver, 1766

The bays of the lake and the shores of rivers supply great quantities of wild rice. At harvest time the Indians venture with their canoes into the rice paddies. One harvester scoops the head of rice over the boat while another shakes it, causing the grain to fall into the canoe.

Joseph N. Nicollet, 1836

Legend of Wild Rice

Wenibozho of the Chippewas and his grandmother, Nokomis, lived together in a lodge by themselves. When he approached manhood his grandmother exhorted him to exert himself, to learn to endure hardship, loneliness, cold and hunger and thirst, for such experience is the proper training for a young man. A young man needs such training so that when overtaken by misfortune he shall be brave and resourceful, so that he may be able to take care of himself and of any who may be dependent upon him.

So one day Wenibozho told his grandmother he was going away into the wilderness where he had never been before, so that he could be cast upon his own resources to try his strength and courage and wit.

He was gone many days and nights, wandering through the forest and beside streams and lakes. He subsisted upon such fruits, seeds, roots and tubers as he was able to find, and upon the flesh of animals he was able to shoot with his bow and arrows which he had brought with him. One day he came to a lake in which was growing a great quantity of beautiful, feathery wild rice, swaying over the water in the gentle breeze. From the bark of a birch tree he fashioned a canoe in which he rowed out upon the lake and gathered a quantity of the wild rice. He did not know the wild rice was useful for food, for he had never seen it before, but he admired its beauty. He took to his grandmother the wild rice which he had gathered. He told her that he had found this beautiful plant in the lake and that he had brought to her some of the seed of the plant. This seed they sowed in another lake, near the place where they live, for Wenibozho hoped to have the plant growing where he might often enjoy its beauty.

Melvin R. Gilmore, *Prairie Smoke*

Minnesota Voyageur Wild Rice Turkey Casserole

Turkey, wild, and later domestic, was a Christmas staple long before Thanksgiving made it obligatory and one aspect of such a Christmas feast is the "leavings." We honor the spirit of our fore-mothers in the use and reuse of the turkey leftover. Thrifty by nature or not a pioneer cook could not afford to use such a treat just once. This recipe combines the fowl with Minnesota wild rice and a pinch of rosemary to elevate a leftover to distinction.

To begin, wash and clean, draining thoroughly, *1 c. wild rice* and *1 c. brown rice;* put in a pot with *6 c. water* and *1 tsp. salt.* Bring to boil then simmer for 1 hour or until all liquid is absorbed. If it has boiled too fast add a little water so wild rice kernels end up looking "popped" and fluffy.

Meanwhile, clean turkey carcass and amass at least *3 c. turkey,* set aside. Chop *1½ c. celery* and *1 medium onion* and using *2 tbsp. butter* or *margarine* sauté over low heat until soft but not soggy. Combine turkey, celery, and onion with *1-4 oz. can of mushrooms* using liquid; add *1 c. coarsely chopped slivered almonds* and *1 tsp. to 1 tbsp. dried rosemary* (depending on your familiarity with and fondness for this herb). Mix the turkey combination with the cooked rices using *1 can cream of chicken soup* and *1 c. of sour cream (half* or *all plain yogurt* may be sub-stituted). Put in a large casserole topping with *bread crumbs* and a sprinkling of *dried parsley,* or *grated parmesan cheese.* Bake in 350 degree oven 30-40 minutes.

TRE

A Christmas Fable

The greedy turkey gobbled up the goodly fare and grew fatter day by day, but the prudent turkey, suspicious of such bountiful grub, refused to eat it and grew rapidly thinner. Finally the master came and said: "Better keep the fat turkey for Christmas: if we do not kill the thin turkey he may die on our hands."
Moral.—Enjoy the good things of life as they come.

The Prison Mirror, Stillwater, Minnesota
December, 1882

Cranberries

The berries which the Ojibway call "mashki gimin" are, however, of still greater value to them; . . . The English call them "cranberries," but they are much larger and finer than our fruit of that name. They grow in swamps, and are ripe in October. I was told that half the Indian families then absent from the village had gone "dans les ottakas," or to the cranberry harvest. All the Canadian, British, and American settlers along this river also preserve large quantities of this pleasant bitter-sweet and refreshing berry. It has recently become a valuable article to export to Lower Canada and America, and one of the settlers boasted that he exported several tons annually. The poor Indians have to do the principal work: they go off with squaw and children into the swamp, often forty miles away, build a temporary shelter there, and pick as many berries as they can. The "great preservers" on the river then buy their harvest of them. Although the berries are ripe in October, it is always better to pluck them later in winter. The fruit has, namely, the peculiarity that it does not fall off of itself; it remains on the branch, and will go on ripening even beneath the snow. The old berries may be seen still on the bush when the new leaves and blossom are already put forth. These ottakas do not require drying or preserving, for they keep through the whole winter in the Indian lodges, and are for a long time as fresh as if just plucked from the tree.

Johann George Kohl, *Kitchi-gami, Life Among the Lake Superior Ojibway*

🌿   🌿   🌿

I was the first white woman in Eden Prairie. I came in 1854 with my husband and small children and settled there in one of the first log houses built. We paid for our farm the first year, from the cranberries which grew in a bog on our land and which we sold for $1.00 a bushel.

Mrs. Robert Anderson, 1854

The only fruit we had for winter use was dried apples, wild plums, wild crab apples and cranberries. In the season, we had wild berries which were very plentiful. There was a cranberry marsh a half mile west of Lake Calhoun, on what is now Lake Street, where we used to go to gather berries. One day a party of four drove to the marsh and just as we were about to alight, we saw that a large buck had taken possession of our field. We did not dispute his claim, but silently stole away.

Charles M. Loring, 1860

Cranberry Compote

Place *2 c. sugar* and *2 c. water* into a saucepan. Stir until the sugar dissolves and boil for 5 minutes. Then add *1 lb. (4 c.) choice cranberries* and simmer in the syrup, without covering the pan, for about five minutes. Add the *grated rind of an orange,* then pour into a large mold which has been rinsed in cold water. Chill until firm. Unmold to serve.

TRE

Frontier Fruit Cake

Three cups of dried apples, wash and cut each piece into three pieces, then boil in a syrup made of *2 c. of sugar, ½ c. of water, 2 tbsp. of essence of lemon,* until preserved through and tender. Be very careful not to let it burn. When cooked sufficiently, take off and cool; then add *1 c. of dried cherries, 3 c. of raisins, 2 c. of sugar, ½ c. of brandy, 1 c. of butter, 6 eggs, 1 tsp. of cloves, nutmeg and cinnamon,* pulverized and mixed; *flour* to make a stiff batter; bake one hour.

Coffee, Not Slops

It is easier to make good coffee than poor. Roast but a little at a time. See that it is cooked, not burnt. Do not grind it too fine, wet it to a paste consistency with clear cold water. Put in the white of an egg, or a piece of cod fish skin to settle it. Put in as much cold water as you want coffee. Put it over a hot fire so it will quickly boil—and do not let it boil more than sixty seconds, or you lose the essence of the coffee by evaporation. If boiled too long you have a muddy slop instead of clear coffee.

The St. Cloud Journal, December 14, 1872

Christmas Eve around a Civil War Camp Fire

As rations were yet very scarce, we were informed that a short distance below Savannah were several large oyster-beds. A detail of two men and two teams went down to see if it was possible to procure enough for a Christmas dinner in the regiment.

On their return we found they had succeeded in filling one of the wagon boxes, but they were of a very inferior quality. The natives called them "cluster oysters." There were two to five in one bunch, and hard to get out. So our Christmas dinner did not consist of turkey with oyster filling and cranberry sauce.

What a glorious camp fire we had that Christmas Eve of 1863! It makes me rub my hands together to think of it. The nights were getting cold and frosty, so that it was impossible to sleep under our little shelter-tents, with comfort; and so, half of the night we spent around the blazing fires in front of our tents.

I always took care that there should be a blazing good fire for our little squad, anyhow. My duties were light and left me time, which I found I could spend with pleasure in swinging an axe. Hickory and white-oak saplings were my favorites, and I had them piled up as high as my head on wooden fire-dogs. What a glorious crackle we had by midnight!

We could go out to the fire at any time of night we pleased (and we were pretty sure to go out three or four times a night, for it was too cold to sleep in the tent more than an hour at a stretch), and we would always find half a dozen of the boys sitting about the fire logs, smoking their pipes, telling yarns, or singing snatches of old songs.

It was hard to be homeless at this merry season of the year, when folks up North were having such happy times, wasn't it? But it was wonderful how elastic the spirits of our soldiers were, and how jolly they could be under the most adverse circumstances. . . .

William Bircher, *A Drummer Boy's Diary, 1861-1865*, St. Paul

Christmas Bells

by Henry Wadsworth Longfellow

Longfellow was a popular nineteenth-century poet best known for his narrative poems based on American folk legends such as The Song of Hiawatha *and* The Courtship of Miles Standish. *This selection and the one which follows by Robert Bly are Christmas poems concerned with the tragedy of war.* Christmas Bells *was written in 1863 after Longfellow's son was wounded in the Civil War.*

I heard the bells on Christmas Day
Their old, familiar carols play,
    And wild and sweet
    The words repeat
Of peace on earth, good-will to men!

And thought how, as the day had come,
The belfries of all Christendom
    Had rolled along
    The unbroken song
Of peace on earth, good-will to men!

Till, ringing, swinging on its way,
The world revolved from night to day
    A voice, a chime,
    A chant sublime
Of peace on earth, good-will to men!

Then from each black, accursed mouth
The cannon thundered in the South
    And with the sound
    The carols drowned
Of peace on earth, good-will to men!

It was as if an earthquake rent
The hearth-stones of a continent,
    And made forlorn
    The households born
Of peace on earth, good-will to men!

And in despair I bowed my head;
"There is no peace on earth," I said;

"For hate is strong
   And mocks the song
Of peace on earth, good-will to men!"

Then pealed the bells more loud and deep,
"God is not dead; nor doth He sleep!
   The Wrong shall fail,
   The Right prevail,
Of peace on earth, good-will to men!"

Christmas Eve Service at Midnight at St. Michael's

by Robert Bly

A cold night; the sidewalk we walk on icy; the dark surrounds the frail wood houses that were so recently trees. We left my father's house an hour before midnight, carrying boxes of gifts out to the car. My brother, who had been killed six months before, was absent. We had wept sitting near the decorated tree. Now I see the angel on the right of St. Michael's altar kneeling on one knee, a hand pressed to his chin. The long-needled Christmas pine, who is the being inside us who is green both summer and winter, is hung with red ribbons of triumph. And it is hung with thirty golden balls, each ball representing a separate planet on which that eternal one has found a home. Outdoors the snow labors its old Manichean labors to keep the father and his animals in melancholy. We sing. At midnight the priest walks down one or two steps, finds the infant Christ, and puts him into the cradle beneath the altar, where the horses and the sheep have been waiting.

Just after midnight, he turns to face the congregation, lifts up the dry wafer and breaks it—a clear and terrifying sound. He holds up the two halves . . . frightening . . . like so many acts, it is permanent. With his arms spread, the cross clear on his white chasuble, he tells us that Christ intended to leave his body behind. It is confusing . . . we take our bodies with us when we go. I see oceans dark and lifting near flights of stairs, oceans lifting and torn over which the invisible birds drift like husks over November roads. . . . The cups are put down. The ocean has been stirred and calmed. A large man is flying over the water with wings spread, a wound on his chest.

Born in Madison, Minnesota, poet Robert Bly is the author of numerous books for which he has received many honors including the National Book Award and a Fulbright Fellowship. He is known as well for his activism in the Vietnam era and as a founder of American Writers Against the Vietnam War.

An Indian man once told us the following tale: "When one of our old men who died arrived at the land of souls, he first met some Frenchmen who greeted him and gave him a hearty welcome. He then reached the place where the Indians are. They also received him very well. Every day there were feasts, to which the French usually were invited because in the land of souls there never are quarrels or wars between them. After the old man had seen all this, he returned and reported it to his tribesmen."

Father Louis Hennepin, 1680

Santa's Show
Thomas Nast, 1890

CHRISTMAS IS COMING

Long Underwear and Such Things
by Clarice Olson Adelmann

During winter, Dame Fashion was a stranger to all of us. Style took a back seat since we dressed with just one objective in mind—to keep from freezing to death.

Awakening in our chill bedroom on school mornings, we found frost thick on the windows. From the front room came the comforting sound of woodchunks shifting in the potbellied heater, and we knew that the freshly stoked fire had taken hold enough to make dressing possible. Teeth chattering, we sprinted to the stove, jockeying for position close to the heat. Throwing all modesty to the winds, we dressed side by side as rapidly as our numbed fingers allowed. First the long underwear, with the three-button rear flap, inevitably missing a button or two with a resultant droop, then for us girls the long brown cotton stockings which had to be anchored somewhere around the thigh with safety pins. How we hated the lumpy underwear showing through the stockings! Worse yet, the law of gravity came into play, so that when we bent over, the sagging seats of our long johns were visible to one and all.

After the usual hurried breakfast of cream and bread, it was time to prepare for the trek to school. A mad scramble ensued as we got ready to face the outdoors. Scratchy wool snowpants and coats went on first, then four-buckle overshoes with only one buckle, or for some, snap overshoes with snaps that refused to snap. If one had recently grown into a new shoe size, it was necessary to wear a pair of boots outgrown by a sibling but too large for the new owner, the fit improved somewhat by stuffing newspapers into the toes. Various caps and scarves mummified us, and we stopped last at the food-warming compartment above the cookstove, which for us was not a food-warming compartment at all, but a place where stiff and frozen mittens were dried and warmed up. It was an unusually fortunate child who found a matched pair; to find two that weren't missing thumbs was a stroke of luck in itself. Dad's wool socks served nicely as liners. Thus prepared to battle the cold, off we trudged into the blinding early morning sun, eyes tearing, with the unrelenting north wind whipping at our small figures—a rather colorful if unstylish troop intent on reaching the drafty one-room schoolhouse a mile and half away. All this, of course, providing that the temperature was no colder than -20 degrees. In our district, school was not in session if the thermometer dipped any lower.

For Dad, however, there was no such hiatus. No matter how cold it became, the livestock still needed tending, the barn needed cleaning, and the milking had to be done. His outfit, consequently, was designed to provide maximum protection. First, of course, the long underwear, then a pair of old pants from a wool suit, followed by one or sometimes two pair of overalls. On his feet, he wore wool socks, a pair of felt shoes and overshoes. (He swore felt shoes were the warmest foot covering one could have.) Atop his heavy flannel shirt, he put on a sheepskin vest and a Mackinaw jacket, covered his head with a sheepskin cap with warm earflaps, and protected his hands with wool liners inside of cowhide mittens. This was his "going to town" outfit, too, as it was for most farmers in the area. The only concession he made to venturing onto the cosmopolitan scene was to wipe some, but never all, of the barnyard offal from his overshoes before the trip. It would have been considered sheer idiocy, let along unforgettable vanity, for one to attempt the fifteen-mile trip in the Model-A along the wind-swept gravel roads of the frigid prairie without such attire.

Mom, during that time of year, for the most part stayed snug in our little house, except for her forays out to check on her beloved chickens that only occasionally during the bitter cold deigned to present her with a welcome egg or two. Her garb included the usual long underwear, lisle stockings, housedress, an old wool coat and one of Dad's caps.

Vogue would have sniffed at our getups. All the same, our homely outfits served in the struggle against the elements. We had about us, I think, a certain look of élan!

Shortly after Thanksgiving, we prepared to celebrate Christmas. Evergreens were not native to our woods and to pay money for a tree, of all things, was not to be considered. Instead, we strung two paper garlands, one red and one green, from one corner of the small front room to the other. On the windows, we pasted cut-out snowflakes, thus completing the business of decorating in short order.

Good smells perfumed the kitchen—molasses cookies and sugar cookies, *fattigmans* bubbling in deep fat, and lefse browning in large circles on the cookstove. The kettle of sweet soup simmered, the dizzying fragrance of prunes, raisins, and apricots mixing with that of the spices.

Dad brought from a town a wooden pail of *sil* (herring), and of course the lutefisk for Christmas Eve. He brought, too, a box of apples which was shoved beneath our bed—a stroke of luck. (I learned later that the storage place for the fruit was not an accident. Dad simply could not bring himself to give a present. Far more comfortable a situation was for him to complain over the crunching sounds emanating from our room after the house was dark.)

A week or so before Christmas was the program at our country church, the high point of the Yuletide season. Our parents saw to it that we sported new clothes for the occasion, determined that we should not shame them by our appearance on the big night.

We were told early in life that Santa Claus did not exist; consequently, we did not expect toys. Deep inside, though, we wished that the folks would be proven wrong. With a mixture of hope and half-heartedness, we each hung one brown stocking near the heating stove on Christmas Eve. In the morning we found a modest gift stuffed into the sock—perhaps a pair of mittens or a cap. There was one year which proved an exception, when Mom smilingly presented us with a game of Chinese checkers, cause for jubilance amongst us. For years after, the metal playing board and marbles provided amusement during the long winter hours spent indoors.

❧   ❧   ❧

Fattigman

A traditional Scandinavian Christmas treat, fattigman is a fried not baked cookie. Under other names such as "poor man's cookie," similar recipes are native to the Germans, Italians, and Eastern Europeans.

Beat *4 egg yolks* well, add *4 tbsp. sugar* and beat again. Add *1 tbsp. hot water* and continue beating until light. Now add *4 tbsp. sweet or sour cream, 1½ c. flour,* and *a pinch of salt.* Chill dough. Then roll quite thin, ⅛ inch or less. Cut in diamond shape and slit the center; pull one end of the dough through the slit. Fry in hot oil 350° only a few at a time, until light brown. This takes less than a minute. Remove from fat with a slotted spoon and drain on paper towels. Sprinkle with sugar while warm, or allow to cool slightly and dust with powdered sugar. Store in airtight tin when thoroughly cool, or freeze.

TRE

Christmas in those hard times did not mean to us little pioneer children what it does now. There was no spare money with which to buy presents. We always hung up our stockings, but got nothing in them but a little cheap candy, and perhaps a few raisins. But one year, father determined to give us and the other children of the village a little better Christmas than usual. So he went out to his woods and cut enough fire wood to exchange in St. Cloud for a barrel of apples. Then he divided off one end of our sitting room with a sheet and arranged a puppet show behind it. And with the village children in one end of the room eating apples, and father in the other managing the puppets, we celebrated the day in a very happy way.

Mrs. W. L. Neimann, 1857

A Country School Christmas

by Britania J. Livingston

The following account by a pioneer woman describes a country school Christmas during the years after the Civil War.

It was a very commonplace neighborhood. It was composed of the families of hard working farmers, and had hardly emerged from the chrysallis "frontier." Going to the school house on Sabbath afternoons to hear some minister from town preach upon the sins of Free Masonry or the evils of too luxurious living was about their only recreation. As Christmas drew near, the little ones would canvas the prospect of getting their stockings filled by Santa Claus, and thrifty papas would remind the eager darlings that it had been a bad year for Santa Claus' business; that they had heard that he was near stopping his business and closing out at auction, and other nonsense of this same kind.

How it ever came about I am sure I cannot tell. It was arranged to have a Christmas tree at the school house.

The most of the children had never seen a real Christmas tree. The idea started between the teacher and two or three ladies—perhaps it was evolved by a sort of mental spontaneous combustion. It was spoken of only a week before Christmas. The weather was so bad—snowy and blustering—that no committee could get their heads together for consultation; but during that week after school hours, the fine floury snow of Minnesota was melted off the trim overcoat of "our teacher" beside nearly every hot stove in his school district.

And here I must explain who "our teacher" was, and then you will better understand his interest in the matter. He belonged to the neighborhood. He had grown up with the younger people—had received his education at the same schoolhouse where he was now teaching—barring a few terms away at college. He was such a favorite with the parents that he could have the school whenever he wished it, at the highest price going. He petted the little boys as though every little cub was his brother, and he was the idol of the sweetest bevy of maidens under ten years of age, that ever graced a country neighborhood. Said he, of a general summing up of the undertaking. "We are all in the same boat, there will be no costly presents to disturb the harmony. If we can give the little ones a good time, the rest of us will certainly be happy. The large boys have chipped in to get a barrel of apples, and I think we are sure of a pleasant evening." When they struck that barrel of apples they were sure of one element of success—a crowd. A "barrel of apples" is an inducement beyond the power of the average Minnesotan to resist.

So it was a settled thing about the tree. Then every mother laid her plans to help Santa Claus. As I said before, consultation was impossible, so Mrs. H. counted up the little children that were sure to be there, and found that they numbered twenty. So that every child should certainly have something, she cut twenty stockings out of blue mosquito netting, made them neatly and wrote each child's name and fastened it to the stocking, and then made a few extra ones for any extra children that might happen to come.

Mrs. S., with the same thoughtful purpose, counted also, and made twenty little stockings and a few extra ones, and pinned on the names with only this difference—the mosquito bar was pink. Mrs. P., not knowing the counting and planning going on at the snow-bound neighbors, counted also, and made neat little white bags with fancy strings for twenty. Mrs. L. did the same thing. So you can see for yourself that the thing was a success from the start. But wait: the teacher has not done all of his part yet. Fearing that some might be slighted or overlooked by the saint, in a crowded house, he went to town counting as he rode along, up to twenty, and he invested in twenty toys.

How many mothers set the children to popping corn, each one fancying she was the only one who possessed any, or the knowledge necessary to make it into balls. There were certainly bushels of it piled up under the tree in pans and baskets, in the shape of balls. When every available use had been made of the dry corn, even to filling new boots with it, the remainder was tied up in a cloth flour sack, the name of a very goodnatured man written on it, and then hung up to the stovepipe.

Christmas evening was clear and beautiful. All day long the teacher and his aids were at the school house arranging the tree, the ever-green decorations, and receiving those who came on business.

Did you ever witness the delight of a lot of children on their view of a Christmas tree? If not I am sorry for you.

At "early candle light" the sleigh bells began to ring up their merry loads. The school house was crowded to an overflow. Of course the tree committee had its heaviest work at the last minute. Then while the teacher ran home to wash off the perspiration and get on a clean collar, we had time to look around.

A brighter, prettier tree we never saw, although we have looked on those of ten times the value. It was a graceful red cedar, well lighted with candles and well loaded with presents, as was also a table nearby, and the floor at its roots. Opposite between the two windows was a very emphatic picture of "Saint Nick" in very gay colors, on a tidy I suspect, although four year old Robbie declared it was a handkerchief and that he must have it.

On every suitable place upon the walls were pictures and sentiments suitable to the occasion, while over all were green branches of the fragrant red cedar, and clusters of the pretty bittersweet berries in lieu of the sacred holly. Beneath all were the bright eyes of the happy children, and gratified faces of their parents. We could not help but notice little Robbie W. His mamma tried to keep him down, but up on the seat he would pop, like a Jack-in-a-box when the cover is off.

Who will be Santa Claus? was the all important query. No one thought of the teacher, for, have I said so? he was the most bashful man you ever knew. Why, when he was a great boy of eighteen years, if you stopped to speak to him, his arms and legs would try to get out of sight, and he had every appearance of a man trying to hide behind himself. Of course he has gotten over all that, and stands straight as a liberty pole, and looks squarely at you with a firm blue eye. Yet he still prefers to do his good works in private—always pushing someone to the front, with half his brains and three times his brass, when a public stand is to be taken. But he has forgotten himself tonight—you can see that as he carefully picks his way through the crowd of little ones that clutch at his hands and his coat-tails as he passes, each one of them with some private word to whisper in his ear.

When near the tree, he faced around and said: "I suppose you all know why we have gathered here," pointing to the beautiful tree. "The first exercise will be a little vocal music, after which some of the little ones will give recitations suitable to the evening."

That sweet hymn, "Peace Upon Earth, the Angels Sing" never sounded sweeter than in that little old schoolhouse that Christmas night. The little ones spoke like the angels whose messengers they are. Then two little girls were chosen to carry the presents to their recipients, and two young men took them from the tree and handed them to the teacher who read out the name and gave to the little messengers for the owners.

The "twenty" soon had received their pairs of pink and blue stockings which Santa Claus has filled with candies, nuts, maple sugar, etc., and the children that were unexpected had their names called and were served just as well as the others. Then if the tree had been emptied I think those little ones would always have blessed it. But it was still loaded, such sights of pretty mittens, suspenders, leggings, neckties, slippers, dolls, drums, dolls' clothing, books, pictures, and several pairs of small boots and hoods. O, I cannot begin to mention the things. Nothing costly, nearly everything useful, but so bright and handsome. Suspended by threads to the tree in such a manner as to keep quivering and dancing were two or three jumping jacks whose gesticulations attracted all eyes. As one of these was handed to the teacher, he pulled the string and made it dance worse than ever. "That is what I want," shouted four year old Robbie. "No, Robbie, you can't have this," said the teacher, "this is for our postmaster." The shouts of laughter didn't quite drown Robbie's disgusted "pshaw." It is needless to say that the P. M. is a man who enjoys a good laugh, if it does happen to be against himself.

In the crowd was a man who had not heard of the tree till nearly evening—his children had enjoyed their full stockings, but he thought they would enjoy the ride and seeing the tree, so he brought them over four miles. "The three M's," he called his little ones. Mary, Mattie and Mand, we believe. We saw the delight of the little ones when their names were called and a stockie full of candies was handed each of them. Hanging on one of the outermost twigs of the tree, was a pair of the cutest baby socks, pure white, filled with candy and labeled "for the smallest baby in the room." After a little animated discussion the stockies were given to the youngest "M" just six weeks old. As the mother drew them over the sweet pink toes, she looked as pleased over the unexpected present as she would as an "expected" one of much greater value.

Pans of popcorn balls passed around and refreshments became the order of the evening. All this time the tree was being stripped of its precious fruit as fast as circumstances would permit. "Here, Robbie," called the teacher, holding up a bright tin pail. "This pail has your name on it. It has got something in it, too. I can hear it rattle," shaking the pail gently and lifting up the cover to peep in it. "Shut it up!" yelled Robbie, then settled back alarmed at the shouting and stamping aroused by his impulsive speech. "Just what I wanted, anyway teacher," when he found his voice again and had looked into his precious pail. But our little fellow's happiness was complete when one of the committee on taking down one of the jumping-jacks found his own name on it, slyly nipped it off and put Robbie's in its place. "Now let us go home," he said. "I'm all ready, I've got what I want."

Pop Corn Balls

While popping your corn put some syrup on the stove, the nicer the better, and boil it down quite thick. Put your corn while hot in a dish pan, or any large vessel convenient, pour the syrup over it, and stir it well with a spoon. It only needs enough to make the corn stick together. Butter your fingers and make up the balls quickly, any size you wish. Lay on a plate until cool and they are nice especially on a winter night when young people are sparking.

St. Cloud Journal, Dec. 14, 1872

I remember practicing for our Christmas program from Thanksgiving on. On the night of the performance, the sight of the lighted schoolhouse caused flutters in my stomach. It was always a thrill getting a box of three pencils with my name on them from the teacher.

Alice L. Soffa, *Country School Memories*

School holidays were listed on the contract, as was the need to have Christmas programs. There were corn picking and seeding vacations, so we really managed only eight months of school.

For the Christmas program, a stage was set up with blocks, and planks were laid across them. Some schools had old curtains. If not, sheets were used. They sagged, wires broke, and down came the curtains! A placard with instuctions was fastened with rope, so all the pupils had to do was walk on, follow the directions, and walk off. Children drew names and gifts were exchanged. Teachers gave a gift to each child and received one in return. Apples, which were furnished by the school board, were passed out to the audience. Teachers filled the children's sacks with goodies.

Arlie M. Klimes, *Country School Memories*

We always had a Christmas program for our parents. We had a big Christmas tree, on which we put real candles. We lit the candles on the night of our program when the schoolroom was packed with people. As I remember those Christmas trees, I still shake my head and wonder how we dared to do such a thing. We were so lucky.

Selma Anderson Hughes, *Country School Memories*

All social life—Christmas programs, social picnics, school plays, community clubs—revolved around the schoolhouse as the one meeting place available. When the country school went, much of the rural social life disintegrated. Its common center, the school, was no more.

From Milton S. Johnson, *Country School Memories*

A Wisit From St. Nicholas
Plagiarism, Norwegian-style
by Dave Wood

Before I began working full time for the Minneapolis Tribune in 1981, I contributed occasional pieces to the editorial-opinion pages, many of which I wrote in Scandinavian dialect. I have little chance to do that these days, but this Christmas I tried my hand at some derivative verse. Try reading it aloud, exactly the way it's spelled, and you could make a hit at your next Sons of Norway banquet:

Vuss da nate before Chrissmuss, an' all trew da house,
Not ing-a-ting vuss stirring, not ee-wenn a mouse.
Da jung vunss vuss packed lake sardeence in vun bed
Vile wish-unss uff rommegrot danced in dare head.

Ma, she cooked lew-ta-fisk in a nightgown of puce.
And me? Ay yusst sucked on a big cud uff snoose.
Den over da hoghouse aroce such a cladder,
Ay yumped from da tee-vee tew see vhut vuss da madder.

Avay tew da front porch ay tromped in may bewtss
Lake Ingvald, da hired man, on one uff his tewtss.
Den vhut tew may vundering ice should appear?
A Yohn Deere corn binder, pulled by eight vite-tail deer.

Vid a little old drifer so nimble an' kvik,
Dat I sviftly de-dewced dat he musst be St. Nick.
Fasster den Pug Lund, da vite-tailss day came,
An' he visseled and shouted and called dem by name:

"Now Astrid! Now Birgit! Now Rundvig an' Ragne!
On Torbjorn! On Torsten! On Ole an' Magne!
Pass da manure pile, get on da ball,
Speed tew da farmhouse and climb op da vall!"

An' den in a tah-vinkling ay heard on our rewf
Da prancing an' pawing uff each little hewf.
Ay vent tew da fireplace tew trow on a stick,
An' down trew da shimney slid yolly St. Nick.

Hiss eyes day vuss blue, hiss smile it ver sveet,
Hiss nose vuss bright red from tew much aquavit.
Hiss cap vuss from Monkey Vord, his bewts verr Sears' Best
An' hiss bundle uff gifts put hiss back tew da test:

A krumkake baker, for Inger, my vife.
For me, a Rapala fish-cleaning knife.
Ski poles for Sven (pluss a novel by Undset).
For Lena? Membership in Nordmann's Forbundet.

Nick didn't make small talk, tewk giftss from hiss sack,
Lake Hadacol for Grandma an' her miss-rub-bel hack.
A truss for poor Leroy, for Ingvald some schnapps,
And for Ole a "buster fuzz" tew vord off da copss.

He hitched op hiss trouserss, viped his noce on hiss sleeve,
Consulted hiss sked-yewl, said "Yee I gotta leeve."
Den, laying hiss finger inside uff his lip,
Nick dug out vet snoose, den gave it a flip.

He sprang tew da binder, tew da deer gafe a vissel
An' away day all flew, lake a Pershing crewce missile.
Ay heard him giff holler, ass he drofe out uff sight,
"Ya, Glad Jul tew all, and tew all a gewd night."

After a 20-year career as a college English professor, Dave Wood became a full-time journalist. He is currently the book editor for the Star and Tribune *newspaper of the Twin Cities and author of* Wisconsin Life Trip, Telling Tales Out of School, *and co-author of* The Pie Lady of Winthrop. *His most recent book is* My Mother the Arsonist.

A Christmas Eve Visit by Angels to Stillwater Prison

Well Dan, thet clangin' bell hes tapped, the
    'lectric lites is out.
Ther' aint no sound excepin' of the nite
    gards crepin' 'bout.
It's Crismus eve, an' tho' the day hes been
    all dark an' drear,
Sumthin' come this afternoon thet bro't a
    thankful tear.

The Wimmin's Temp'rence Union from up
    at Fairy'bo,
Sent me a bran new handkercher es white
    es driftin' snow.
I did'nt hope fer sich es thet, it made my
    old eyes wet,
To think them Christian wimmin did'nt
    such as me forget.

An' so it set me thinkin' Dan, ov why thet
    they shud do
A fr'endly act ov thet kind, fer sech as me
    an' you.
An' I reckon it wuz Jesus Christ, thet made
    them do th' deed.
An' I reckon thet they knew that they wuz
    sowin' ov good seed.

Well a gettin' ov thet present, it reminded
    me ov home.
How we set an' waited Crismus eve fur
    Santa Claus to come.
How we hung the stockin's grandma knit,
    beside the chimbly place.
With smiles of pleasure shinin' out on
    every happy face.

It 'minded me ov mother when she told
    about the star
Thet hovered over Jesus in thet land away
    so far.

How they found him in the manger layin' on
    his mother's breast,
An' thet if we wud but love him we could
    find eternal rest.
Then my tho'ts went on to manhood in the
    day I took a wife,
To the little child thet com along to com-
    fort ov my life.
To her sweet blue eyes wide open es she
    herd what I wud say
When I spoke to her ov Santa Claus, an'
    told ov Crismus day.
How one Crismus eve I dressed her in her
    nitegown spotless white.
How she hugged me close an' whispered—
    "Dear, sweet papa, nitey-nite."
How in the mornin' when she waked, her
    heart wuz full ov glee,
Fer Santa Claus hed cum along an' left a
    Crismus tree.
An' thinkin' ov one little child, another
    cum to mind,
The sweetest child Eternal God in heaven
    or earth cud find.
Of the little baby, Jesus, born so long ago
    to-nite,
The gentle, loving Saviour, up in heaven's
    home so brite.
Then sad tho'ts of poor old mother, cum
    into my head an' went,
And saw her brown eyes full of tears, her
    head in sorrow bent,
But I knew this blessed Jesus, He wud fill
    her heart with joy,
An' make it light fer her to live without her
    youngest boy.
So God bless them temp'rance wimmin fer
    rememberin' sech as we,

May the angels guide them every one, safe
 o'er the crystal sea,
May they h'eve a crown in glory an' a home
 among the blest!
May they find a place to lay the'r heads
 upon the Saviour's breast.

Prison Mirror, Stillwater, Minnesota
December, 1887

Christmas Memories: Roseau, Minnesota
by Anna Rice Turngren

I like Christmas for all the memories it brings to mind: the music, the food and, best of all, family stories of years past in Roseau, Minnesota.

I remember a poignant incident involving the youngest of my six siblings, Erling, who was thirteen years my junior. The year he was six, as Christmas drew closer, he seemed very anxious about something. He was very glad when he was allowed to accompany me uptown to run errands for our mother. With a chance to have a private conversation, he told me he needed my help. He confessed he no longer believed in Santa Claus and was having a hard time pretending he did. He implored me to somehow let the rest of the family know because he couldn't stand putting on an act any longer. I assured him I would talk to the others and that we would have a nice Christmas even though a little child believing in Santa Claus wouldn't be part of it. I guess my brother was relieved to give up the pretense, but I certainly felt sad. A Christmas balloon had burst and we would have to pick up the pieces.

Giving was a central part of my mother's character. She reached out to many people in our small, northern Minnesota town. One year, a couple of months before December, a woman in the neighborhood told my mother how she needed to find a way to earn some extra money to buy food for her family. She hoped to find something she could do in her home, but was having a hard time coming up with an idea. Mama, who was always up on the latest, told her about rag rugs and how popular they were with the townspeople. With just a loom and some rags you could make lovely, practical rugs for every room in the house. Of course, the woman had no money for a loom so my mother gave her enough to buy one for her home-based enterprise.

The months passed and Christmas came. Our family went to church and walked home after the Christmas Eve service. I remember it was a perfect night: the sky was lit with a million candles which shimmered on the snow. As we approached our home, we noticed that someone had been there ahead of us and had left a package by the door. We opened it and found a sturdy, beautiful rag rug. A note was enclosed from Mama's friend thanking her for the loom and telling her that this was the first rug she had made and that she wanted Mama to have it. We all looked at our mother, and then at the rug, realizing that with her giving she had helped someone else to be a giver, too.

Dipping Christmas Candles

I well remember Dipping Candle Day; it was a very interesting day to me in my boyhood, because it was then that the Christmas candle was dipped.

It usually came in the fall, in the short, lonesome days of November, just before the new school-master opened the winter term of the school.

My grandmother brought down from the garret her candle-rods and poles. The candle-rods were light sticks of elder, some fifty in number, and the poles were long pine bars. These poles were tied two each to two chairs, and the rods, after they had been wicked, were laid upon them at short distances apart.

Wicking the candle-rods is a term of which few people to-day know the meaning. Every country store in old times contained a large supply of balls of cotton candle-wick. This wick was to be cut, put upon the candle-rods, twisted, and tallowed or waxed, so as to be convenient for dipping.

How many times have I seen my grandmother, on the long November evenings, wicking her candle-rods! She used to do the work, sitting in her easy-chair before the great open fire. One side of the fireplace was usually hung with strings of dried or partly dried apples, and the other with strings of red peppers. Over the fireplace were a gun and the almanac; and on the hearth there were usually, in the evening, a few sweet apples roasting; and at one end of it was the dog, and at the other the cat.

Dipping candles would seem a comical sight to-day. My grandmother used to sit over a great iron kettle of melted tallow, and patiently dip the wicks on the rods into it, until they grew to the size of candles. Each rod contained about five wicks, and these were dipped together. The process was repeated perhaps fifty or more times.

Hezekiah Butterworth, *St. Nicholas Magazine*

Candle Crafts for Schoolchildren

Use old candles or paraffin and melt it in a coffee can in another pan of water, slowly. You may pour it into any kind of greased mold. While wax is still liquid, suspend a piece of waxed string for a wick to the bottom of the center of the mold by attaching the top end of the string to a pencil or knife placed across the top of the mold. Or you can make cute tiny floating candles by pouring wax onto a cookie sheet and cutting it with cookie cutters while still soft. Put wicks into these by using a hot ice pick, or thin nail held with a pliers, to make the hole, and immediately inserting the stiff waxed short wick.

Martha J. Beckman, Clear Lake, Minnesota

🌱   🌱   🌱

Away we go with bells jingling, horses blowing icicles from their nostrils, ladies alternately laughing and screaming, and young men driving like Jehu . . .

Sleigh ride on the Mississippi River from St. Paul to Red Rock, circa 1852

The Christmas Horses

by Laura Ingalls Wilder

Grasshopper weather was strange weather. Even at Thanksgiving, there was no snow.

The door of the dugout was wide open while they ate Thanksgiving dinner. Laura could see across the bare willow-tops, far over the prairie to the place where the sun would go down. There was not one speck of snow. The prairie was like soft yellow fur. The line where it met the sky was not sharp now; it was smudged and blurry.

"Grasshopper weather," Laura thought to herself. She thought of grasshoppers' long, folded wings and their high-jointed hind legs. Their feet were thin and scratchy. Their heads were hard, with large eyes on the corners, and their jaws were tiny and nibbling.

If you caught a grasshopper and held him, and gently poked a green blade of grass into his jaws, they nibbled it fast. They swiftly nibbled in the whole grass blade, till the tip of it went into them and was gone.

Thanksgiving dinner was good. Pa had shot a wild goose for it. Ma had to stew the goose because there was no fireplace, and no oven in the little stove. But she made dumplings in the gravy. There were corn dodgers and mashed potatoes. There were butter, and milk, and stewed dried plums. And three grains of parched corn lay beside each tin plate.

At the first Thanksgiving dinner the poor Pilgrims had had nothing to eat but three parched grains of corn. Then the Indians came and brought them turkeys, so the Pilgrims were thankful.

Now, after they had eaten their good, big Thanksgiving dinner, Laura and Mary could eat their grains of corn and remember the Pilgrims. Parched corn was good. It crackled and crunched, and its taste was sweet and brown.

Then Thanksgiving was past and it was time to think of Christmas. Still there was no snow and no rain. The sky was grey, the prairie was dull, and the winds were cold. But the cold winds blew over the top of the dugout.

"A dugout is snug and cosy," said Ma. "But I do feel like an animal penned up for the winter."

"Never mind, Caroline," Pa said. "We'll have a good house next year." His eyes shone and his voice was like singing. "And good horses, and a buggy to boot! I'll take you riding, dressed up in silks! Think, Caroline—this level, rich land, not a stone or stump to contend with, and only three miles from a railroad! We can sell every grain of wheat we raise!"

Then he ran his fingers through his hair and said, "I do wish I had a team of horses."

"Now, Charles," said Ma. "Here we are, all healthy and safe and snug, with food for the winter. Let's be thankful for what we have."

"I am," Pa said. "But Pete and Bright are too slow for harrowing and harvesting. I've broken up that big field with them, but I can't put it all in wheat, without horses."

Then Laura had a chance to speak without interrupting. She said, "There isn't any fireplace."

"Whatever are you talking about?" Ma asked her.

"Santa Claus," Laura answered.

"Eat your supper, Laura, and let's not cross bridges till we come to them," said Ma.

Laura and Mary knew that Santa Claus could not come down a chimney when there was no chimney. One day Mary asked Ma how Santa Claus could come. Ma did not answer. Instead, she asked, "What do you girls want for Christmas?"

She was ironing. One end of the ironing-board was on the table and the other on the bedstead. Pa had made the bedstead that high, on purpose. Carrie was playing on the bed and Laura and Mary sat at the table. Mary was sorting quilt blocks and Laura was making a little apron for the rag doll, Charlotte. The wind howled overhead and whined in the stovepipe, but there was no snow yet.

Laura said, "I want candy."

"So do I," said Mary, and Carrie cried, "Tandy?"

"And a new winter dress, and a coat, and a hood," said Mary.

"So do I," said Laura. "And a dress for Charlotte, and—"

Ma lifted the iron from the stove and held it out to them. They could test the iron. They licked their fingers and touched them, quicker than quick, to the smooth hot bottom. If it crackled, the iron was hot enough.

"Thank you, Mary and Laura," Ma said. She began carefully

ironing around and over the patches on Pa's shirt. "Do you know what Pa wants for Christmas?"

They did not know.

"Horses," Ma said. "Would you girls like horses?"

Laura and Mary looked at each other.

"I only thought," Ma went on, "if we all wished for horses, and nothing but horses, then maybe—"

Laura felt queer. Horses were everyday; they were not Christmas. If Pa got horses, he would trade for them. Laura could not think of Santa Claus and horses at the same time.

"Ma!" she cried. "There IS a Santa Claus, isn't there?"

"Of course there's a Santa Claus," said Ma. She set the iron on the stove to heat again.

"The older you are, the more you know about Santa Claus," she said. "You are so big now, you know he can't be just one man, don't you? You know he is everywhere on Christmas Eve. He is in the Big Woods, and in Indian Territory, and far away in York State, and here. He comes down all the chimneys at the same time. You know that, don't you?"

"Yes, Ma," said Mary and Laura.

"Well," said Ma. "Then you see—"

"I guess he is like angels," Mary said, slowly. And Laura could see that, just as well as Mary could.

Then Ma told them something else about Santa Claus. He was everywhere, and besides that, he was all the time.

Whenever anyone was unselfish, that was Santa Claus.

Christmas Eve was the time when everybody was unselfish. On that one night, Santa Claus was everywhere, because everybody, all together, stopped being selfish and wanted other people to be happy. And in the morning you saw what that had done.

"If everybody wanted everybody else to be happy, all the time, then would it be Christmas all the time?" Laura asked, and Ma said, "Yes, Laura."

Laura thought about that. So did Mary. They thought, and they looked at each other, and they knew what Ma wanted them to do. She wanted them to wish for nothing but horses for Pa. They looked at each other again and they looked away quickly and they did not say anything. Even Mary, who was always so good, did not say a word.

That night after supper Pa drew Laura and Mary close to him in the crook of his arms. Laura looked up at his face, and then she snuggled against him and said, "Pa."

"What is it, little half-pint of sweet cider?" Pa asked, and Laura said,

"Pa, I want Santa Claus—to bring——"

"What?" Pa asked.

"Horses," said Laura. "If you will let me ride them sometimes."

"So do I!" said Mary. But Laura had said it first.

Pa was surprised. His eyes shone soft and bright at them. "Would you girls really like horses?" he asked them.

"Oh yes, Pa!" they said.

"In that case," said Pa, smiling, "I have an idea that Santa Claus will bring us all a fine team of horses."

That settled it. They would not have any Christmas, only horses. Laura and Mary soberly undressed and soberly buttoned up their nightgowns and tied their nightcap strings. They knelt down together and said,

> "Now I lay me down to sleep,
> I pray the Lord my soul to keep.
> If I should die before I wake
> I pray the Lord my soul to take,

and please bless Pa and Ma and Carrie and everybody and make me a good girl for ever'n'ever, Amen."

Quickly Laura added, in her own head, "And please make me only glad about the Christmas horses, for ever'n'ever amen again."

She climbed into bed and almost right away she was glad. She thought of horses sleek and shining, of how their manes and tails blew in the wind, how they picked up their swift feet and sniffed the air with velvety noses and looked at everything with bright, soft eyes. And Pa would let her ride them.

Pa had tuned his fiddle and now he set it against his shoulder. Overhead the wind went wailing lonely in the cold dark. But in the dugout everything was snug and cosy.

Bits of firelight came through the seams of the stove and twinkled on Ma's steel knitting-needles and tried to catch Pa's elbow. In the shadows the bow was dancing, on the floor Pa's toe was tapping, and the merry music hid the lonely crying of the wind.

The Christmas Cuckoo
An Old World Folk Tale

by Frances Browne

Once upon a time there stood in the midst of a bleak moor, in the North Country, a certain village. All its inhabitants were poor, for their fields were barren, and they had little trade; but the poorest of them all were two brothers called Scrub and Spare, who followed the cobbler's craft. Their hut was built of clay and wattles. The door was low and always open, for there was no window. The roof did not entirely keep out the rain and the only thing comfortable was a wide fireplace, for which the brothers could never find wood enough to make sufficient fire. There they worked in most brotherly friendship, though with little encouragement.

On one unlucky day a new cobbler arrived in the village. He had lived in the capital city of the kingdom and, by his own account, cobbled for the queen and the princesses. His awls were sharp; his lasts were new; he set up his stall in a neat cottage with two windows. The villagers soon found out that one patch of his would outwear two of the brothers'. In short, all the mending left Scrub and Spare, and went to the new cobbler.

The season had been wet and cold, their barley did not ripen well, and the cabbages never half-closed in the garden. So the brothers were poor that winter, and when Christmas came they had nothing to feast on but a barley loaf and a piece of rusty bacon. Worse than that, the snow was very deep and they could get no firewood.

Their hut stood at the end of the village; beyond it spread the bleak moor, now all white and silent. But that moor had once been a forest; great roots of old trees were still to be found in it, loosened form the soil and laid bare by the winds and rains. One of these, a rough, gnarled log, lay hard by their door, the half of it above the snow, and Spare said to his brother:

"Shall we sit here cold on Christmas while the great root lies yonder? Let us chop it up for firewood, the work will make us warm."

"No," said Scrub, "It's not right to chop wood on Christmas, besides, that root is too hard to be broken with any hatchet."

"Hard or not, we must have a fire," replied Spare. "Come, brother, help me in with it. Poor as we are there is nobody in the village will have such a yule log as ours."

Scrub liked a little grandeur, and, in hopes of having a fine yule log, both brothers strained and strove with all their might till, between pulling and pushing, the great old root was safe on the hearth, and beginning to crackle and blaze with the red embers.

In high glee the cobblers sat down to their bread and bacon. The door was shut, for there was nothing but cold moonlight and snow outside; but the hut, strewn with fir boughs and ornamented with holly, looked cheerful as the ruddy blaze flared up and rejoiced their hearts.

Then suddenly from out the blazing root they heard: "Cuckoo! cuckoo!" as plain as ever the spring bird's voice came over the moor on a May morning.

"What is that?" said Scrub, terribly frightened; "it is something bad!"

"Maybe not," said Spare.

And out of the deep hole at the side of the root, which the fire had not reached, flew a large, gray cuckoo, and lit on the table before them. Much as the cobblers had been surprised, they were still more so when it said:

"Good gentlemen, what season is this?"

"It's Christmas," said Spare.

"Then a merry Christmas to you!" said the cuckoo. "I went to sleep in the hollow of that old root one evening last summer, and never woke till the heat of your fire made me think it was summer again. But now since you have burned my lodging, let me stay in your hut till the spring comes around—I only want a hole to sleep in, and when I go on my travels next summer be assured I will bring you some present for your trouble."

"Stay and welcome," said Spare, while Scrub sat wondering if it were something bad or not.

"I'll make you a good warm hole in the thatch," said Spare. "But you must be hungry after that long sleep—here is a slice of barley bread. Come help us to keep Christmas!"

The cuckoo ate up the slice, drank water from a brown jug,

and flew into a snug hole which Spare scooped for it in the thatch of the hut.

Scrub said he was afraid it wouldn't be lucky; but as it slept on and the days passed he forgot his fears.

So the snow melted, the heavy rains came, the cold grew less, the days lengthened, and one sunny morning the brothers were awakened by the cuckoo shouting its own cry to let them know the spring had come.

"Now I'm going on my travels," said the bird, "over the world to tell men of the spring. There is no country where trees bud, or flowers bloom, that I will not cry in before the year goes round. Give me another slice of barley bread to help me on my journey, and tell me what present I shall bring you at the twelvemonth's end."

Scrub would have been angry with his brother for cutting so large a slice, their store of barley being low, but his mind was occupied with what present it would be most prudent to ask for.

"There are two trees hard by the well that lies at the world's end," said the cuckoo, "one of them is called the golden tree, for its leaves are all of beaten gold. Every winter they fall into the well with a sound like scattered coin, and I know not what becomes of them. As for the other, it is always green like a laurel. Some call it the wise, and some the merry, tree. Its leaves never fall, but they that get one of them keep a blithe heart in spite of all misfortunes, and can make themselves as merry in a hut as in a palace."

"Good master cuckoo, bring me a leaf off that tree!" cried Spare.

"Now, brother, don't be a fool!" said Scrub; "think of the leaves of beaten gold! Dear master cuckoo, bring me one of them!"

Before another word could be spoken the cuckoo had flown out of the open door, and was shouting its spring cry over moor and meadow.

The brothers were poorer than ever that year. Nobody would send them a single shoe to mend, and Scrub and Spare would have left the village but for their barley field and their cabbage garden. They sowed their barley, planted their cabbage, and now that their trade was gone, worked in the rich villagers' fields to make out a scanty living.

So the seasons came and passed; spring, summer, harvest, and winter followed each other as they have done from the beginning. At the end of the latter Scrub and Spare had grown so poor and ragged that their old neighbors forgot to invite them to wedding feasts or merrymakings, and the brothers thought the cuckoo had forgotten them, too, when at daybreak on the first of April they heard a hard knocking at their door, and a voice crying:

"Cuckoo! cuckoo! Let me in with my presents!"

Spare ran to open the door, and in came the cuckoo, carrying in one side of its bill a golden leaf larger than that of any tree in the North Country, and in the other side of its bill one like that of the common laurel, only it had a fresher green.

"Here," it said, giving the gold to Scrub and the green to Spare. "It is a long carriage from the world's end. Give me a slice of barley bread, for I must tell the North Country that the spring has come."

Scrub did not grudge the thickness of that slice, though it was cut from their last loaf. So much gold had never been in the cobbler's hands before, and he could not help exulting over his brother.

"See the wisdom of my choice," he said, holding up the large leaf of gold. "As for yours, as good might be plucked from any hedge; I wonder a sensible bird would carry the like so far."

"Good master cobbler," cried the cuckoo, finishing its slice, "your conclusions are more hasty than courteous. If your brother is disappointed this time, I go on the same journey every year, and for your hospitable entertainment will think it no trouble to bring each of you whichever leaf you desire."

"Darling cuckoo," cried Scrub, "bring me a golden one."

And Spare, looking up form the green leaf on which he gazed as though it were a crown jewel, said:

"Be sure to bring me one from the merry tree."

And away flew the cuckoo.

"This is the feast of All Fools, and it ought to be your birthday," said Scrub. "Did ever man fling away such an opportunity of getting rich? Much good your merry leaves will do in the midst of rags and poverty!"

But Spare laughed at him, and answered with quaint old proverbs concerning the cares that come with gold, till Scrub, at length getting angry, vowed his brother was not fit to live with a respectable man; and taking his lasts, his awls, and his golden leaf, he left the wattle hut, and went to tell the villagers.

They were astonished at the folly of Spare, and charmed with Scrub's good sense, particularly when he showed them the golden leaf, and told that the cuckoo would bring him one every spring.

The new cobbler immediately took him into partnership; the greatest people sent him their shoes to mend. Fairfeather, a beautiful village maiden, smiled graciously upon him; and in the course of that summer they were married, with a grand wedding feast, at which the whole village danced except Spare, who was not invited, because the bride could not bear his low-mindedness, and his brother thought him a disgrace to the family.

As for Scrub he established himself with Fairfeather in a cottage close by that of the new cobbler, and quite as fine. There he mended shoes to everybody's satisfaction, had a scarlet coat and a fat goose for dinner on holidays. Fairfeather, too, had a crimson gown, and fine blue ribbons, but neither she nor Scrub was content, for to buy this grandeur the golden leaf had to be broken and parted with piece by piece, so the last morsel was gone before the cuckoo came with another.

Spare lived on in the old hut, and worked in the cabbage garden. (Scrub had got the barley field because he was the elder.) Every day his coat grew more ragged, and the hut more weather-beaten; but people remarked that he never looked sad or sour. And the wonder was that, from the time any one began to keep his company, he or she grew kinder, happier, and more content.

Every first of April the cuckoo came tapping at their doors with the golden leaf for Scrub, and the green for Spare. Fairfeather would have entertained it nobly with wheaten bread and honey, for she had some notion of persuading it to bring two golden leaves instead of one; but the cuckoo flew away to eat barley bread with Spare, saying it was not fit company for fine people, and liked the old hut where it slept so snugly from Christmas till spring.

Scrub spent the golden leaves, and remained always discontented; and Spare kept the merry ones.

I do not know how many years passed in this manner, when a certain great lord, who owned that village, came to the neighborhood. His castle stood on the moor. It was ancient and strong, with high towers and a deep moat. All the country as far as one could see from the highest turret belonged to its lord; but he had not been there for twenty years, and would not have come then, only he was melancholy. And there he lived in a very bad temper. The servants said nothing would please him, and the villagers put on their worst clothes lest he should raise their rents.

But one day in the harvest time His Lordship chanced to meet Spare gathering water cresses as a meadow stream, and fell into talk with the cobbler. How it was nobody could tell, but from that hour the great lord cast away his melancholy. He forgot all his woes, and went about with a noble train, hunting, fishing, and making merry in his hall, where all travelers were entertained, and all the poor were welcome.

This strange story spread through the North Country, and great company come to the cobbler's hut—rich men who had lost their friends, beauties who had grown old, wits who had gone out of fashion—all came to talk with Spare, and, whatever their troubles had been, all went home merry.

The rich gave him presents; the poor gave him thanks. Spare's coat ceased to be ragged, he had bacon with his cabbage, and the villagers began to think there was some sense in him.

By this time his fame had reached the capital city, and even the court. There were a great many discontented people there; and the king had lately fallen into ill humor because a neighboring princess, with seven islands for her dowry, would not marry his eldest son.

So a royal messenger was sent to Spare, with a velvet mantle, a diamond ring, and a command that he should repair to court immediately.

"Tomorrow is the first of April," said Spare, "and I will go with you two hours after sunrise."

The messenger lodged all night at the castle, and the cuckoo came at sunrise with the merry leaf.

"Court is a fine place," it said, when the cobbler told it he was going, "but I cannot come there; they would lay snares and catch me; so be careful of the leaves I have brought you, and give me a farewell slice of barley bread."

Spare was sorry to part with the cuckoo, little as he had of its company, but he gave it a slice which would have broken Scrub's heart in former times, it was so thick and large. And having sewed up the leaves in the lining of his leather doublet, he set out with the messenger on his way to court.

His coming caused great surprise there. Everybody wondered what the king could see in such a common-looking man; but scarcely had His Majesty conversed with him half an hour, when the princess and her seven islands were forgotten and orders given that a feast for all comers should be spread in the banquet hall.

The princes of the blood, the great lords and ladies, the ministers of state after that discoursed with Spare, and the more they talked the lighter grew their hearts, so that such changes had never been seen at court.

The lords forgot their spites and the ladies their envies, the princes and ministers made friends among themselves, and the judges showed no favor.

As for Spare, he had a chamber assigned him in the palace, and a seat at the king's table. One sent him rich robes, and another costly jewels; but in the midst of all his grandeur he still wore the leathern doublet, and continued to live at the king's court, happy and honored, and making all others merry and content.

The Old Homestead—Going Home for the Holidays
Granville Perkins, 1875

A SENSE
OF PLACE

On the Border of Utter Darkness

by O. E. Rölvaag

An endless plain. From Kansas—Illinois, it stretched, far into the Canadian north, God alone knows how far; from the Mississippi River to the western Rockies, miles without number. . . . Endless . . . beginningless.

A grey waste . . . an empty silence . . . a boundless cold. Snow fell; snow flew; a universe of nothing but dead whiteness. Blizzards from out of the northwest raged, swooped down and stirred up a greyish-white fury, impenetrable to human eyes. As soon as these monsters tire, storms from the northeast were sure to come, bringing more snow. . . . "The Lord have mercy! This is awful!" said the folk, for lack of anything else to say.

Monsterlike the Plain lay there—sucked in her breath one week, and the next week blew it out again. Man she scorned; his works she would not brook. . . . She would know, when the time came, how to guard herself and her own against him!

But there was something she did not know. Had it not been for the tiny newcomer, who by mysterious paths had found his way into the settlement on Christmas morning, the monster might have had her way; but the newcomer made a breach in her plans—a vital breach!

Most marvellous it was, a sort of witchery. A thing so pitifully small and birdlike. . . . There was no substance to him, really nothing. Only a bit of tender flesh wrapped in pink silk. . . . But life dwelt in every fibre of it. Yet hardly life—rather the promise of it. Only

75

a twitching and pulling; something that stretched itself out and curled up again—so fine and delicate that one was afraid to touch it with rude hands.

Beret lay in bed with the newcomer beside her. . . . She should have been stiff and cold long ago; she should be lying in another place, a place where those fellows who howled at night could find fresh joints to lick and gnaw. . . . But here she was, still in bed. The button-sized, red-tipped nose dug itself into her breast, pushed in to find a good hold, and then lay still with satisfied little gruntings. The movement hurt her, but it gladdened her heart, too; for all the world she would not have had it otherwise. Life was returning; instead of that stiff, cold horror, Beret's body grew warmer and stronger with every day that passed. And the grunts at her side became more and more insistent. . . . Ah, well, she would have to shift him over, then, so that there might be peace for a moment!

. . . "Thank God, you have food enough for him!" said Per Hansa. . . . "I never saw a youngster with such an appetite!"

When Beret had finally awakened on that Christmas day, she had acted exactly like the old woman in the fairy tale. She lay still, peeping out at her surroundings and asking herself: "Am I still here! Is this me!" . . . She could not believe it, and she would not believe it, either. . . . Hadn't she finished with this place some time ago!

Winter

by Dick Gray

When I've had a particularly fine time doing something—and then it's over—I get an "empty" or sort of an aching feeling in my stomach. I hate to drive away from a pretty view, or end an exciting tennis game, or close the door on a place where special moments have been spent. Pangs of something or another stay with me for a few moments? regrets that the experiences won't happen again? realizations that the years are flowing by? wishes that others could experience these experiences?

Whatever (speaking Minnesota-ese), I have these types of feelings as the summer and fall wind down and winter approaches.

It starts to build by the end of July when the purple martins stir around in flocks, waiting for the last of the young to fly, and then head south en route to Central America for the winter. The goldfinches nesting in August, picking the fluff from milkweed pods, coincides with the goldenrod blooming, sure signs fall is approaching and another fine season is drawing to a close. Come September, the farmers have cut the third crop of alfalfa, the corn is mature and the first good frost dries the ears to the proper point for picking, and special silos have their heated blowers blowing as the fodder is dried for processing and winter storage. I lie in bed at Parley Lake and can hear the blowing and drying from a distant farm all night long. It's a cozy sound, as long as you know what it is.

Minnesota is the theater of seasons, four distinct times with their own happenings and chain of events . For some reason(!), I don't miss winter when it ends, and spring slips into summer and summer sort of blends into fall. But, from fall to winter is when these seasonal changes hit home with the fact that another season is "in the can." As the leaves change color in October and start to fall, so do hopes that the weather will stay as nice as it has been for the past several months. We know what's coming—a hiatus between one year and the next. For me, the "next year" begins early in November because so many things are set at that time in preparation for the coming spring. The period between early November and early April—five months—is a time that is distinct from the rest of the year.

I love winter. That doesn't mean I'm perverse, it just means I accept and join the cold and ice and snow and short days and long nights as necessary steps, as parts of the process making way for another glorious spring-summer-fall period in Minnesota.

As I'm typing this column, waters of the West Upper Lake portion of Lake Minnetonka are lapping at the shoreline 15 feet from my window. Geese have been cruising overhead, barking like a pack of dogs; pied-billed and eared grebes slowly sink into the water when I wave my arms at them; a muskrat and then a mink swim resolutely by in sight of the window, going to and from their feedings in weed beds; and it won't be long before one or more bald eagles show up to pick off the weak and scavenge the dead.

These are the sort of things that cause me to ache when they're gone. I savor the sweetness and crispness of the Fireside apples that mature by late October, but I hate to have them picked for another year. I totally enjoy transplanting young maples from the woods after their leaves have fallen (my transplanting success-percentage is 100% after about 100 trees) but that "window" of time to transplant is so narrow and so fleeting—gone before you're ready for it to leave. There are so many things that can be done between the end of "summer" and the start of "winter," and maybe part of the feeling that I get is due to some measure of frustration at not getting all things done to the extent I wanted.

That's not all bad. Who can expect to accomplish everything, every time?

Nature hangs in there, though, and does her thing at her own pace. She varies somewhat from year to year, but over the millions and jillions of years, her pace averages out and things happen as they should. It's always fascinating to me to observe the same progression of freezing that occurs each year—from small, shallow ponds to along the shores of the small lakes to larger ponds and shallow lakes to the eventual locking in of the rivers and large bodies of water. I tell myself not to forget the code of physics that prevails—that water is heaviest at 39.2 degrees Fahrenheit and as the surface waters cool, they become heavier than the lower warmer waters, and the waters "turn over," preparing the lake or pond for the winter by bringing freshly oxygenated waters to the deeps to allow the fish to survive under the ice and dead algae and weeds to decompose. It's a marvelous mechanism of survival and fundamental to our northern environment.

With the World Series over—and the Twins as World Champs—with hockey and basketball starting up, with the duck season winding down, with leaves being raked and bagged (and I still miss the smell of burning leaves in the fall), with high school football games at their season's end, and with the monarchs gone, the blue-winged and green-winged teal gone, the crows bunching, the blue herons moving (about 100 of them flew past a condo window on the thirteenth floor in Edina on October 31), and the bluebirds flocking (25 in one flock at Parley Lake—nest box success!), you get the funny feeling maybe you're all that's left—you and the rest of man in the North. But then, your friends start pulling out and heading South—to Florida and Arizona, California and Hawaii—and then maybe the feeling becomes one of lonesomeness.

But, no. The grandchildren are still around, the juncos have moved in for the winter, the cardinals and downy, hairy and pileated woodpeckers, the pine siskins and purple finches and goldfinches—all stay with you and come to your feeders all winter long to enrich the wintry scene. They don't let you down. They like the winter, have mastered the techniques of survival, add color and movement to the white and still landscape.

Maybe the feeling I get is one of appreciation, of love for the beauty and thanks for the experiences. These feelings can be experienced most anyplace, but it so happens I get them primarily in Minnesota. I love the place.

> *Dick Gray is a Minneapolis businessman, newspaper columnist, and a founder of the Freshwater Foundation. This organization is devoted to the study of the complex biological problems of freshwater.*

Christmas on the Flats

The Bohemian Flats was a small, isolated community that once lay on the west bank of the Mississippi River in Minneapolis, tucked underneath the Washington Avenue bridge. From the 1880s to the 1940s the village was home to generations of Czech, Polish, Irish, Scandinavian and especially Slovak immigrants. Their story was chronicled by the workers of the Writers' Program of the WPA in a charming history titled The Bohemian Flats.

In the Bohemian Flats as in the old country holidays were closely associated with the church. The Santa Claus myth was not fostered; mothers told their children at Christmas that the Christ child brought the presents. Christmas began on the evening of December 24 and dinner was not served until the stars came out. In many homes a place was set for the family dead because it was felt that they were present on special occasions. Before the dinner was eaten, families partook of holy bread, brought from the church, which they dipped in honey. Some of this bread was also fed to the cows to insure a plentiful supply of milk during the coming year.

Just as the sun was setting and before the church bells rang for the evening service, young girls who wanted to be married began to sweep the kitchen floor. When the first chime of the bell was heard, they would run outside with the sweepings and look about for a man. The name of the first man a girl saw would be the name of the man she would marry. The boys knew the girls would be coming out, so they waited around their doors. "They not only got a kick out of it but often a kiss," laughs a Slovak father. "The best part of the custom was that it really worked!"

After dinner everyone went to the candlelight service at the church. The first Christmas tree on the Flats was set up there and was decorated with tiny candles of twisted wax. An old resident remembers that "we were so afraid the Christmas tree would burn the little church down that we had two men sitting by it all through the service." Carols were sung and the church windows opened wide, so that the light shone on the snow and the songs could be heard far down the street.

Christmas Day was strictly observed. For many years the villagers forbade all work on this day. They could not even sweep the floors. Visiting was postponed until the following day. The only chores permitted were milking and feeding the cows.

Morning services were held at the church. The girls and women did not take seats but stood in front of the altar during the entire service, which frequently lasted two and a half hours. Sometimes a woman fainted before the service was finished, but it was considered disgraceful to sit down. For this occasion older women wore shawls and young married women wore gaily decorated hats, which were later put away until the next Christmas.

The dinner was prepared on the preceding day and typically consisted of mushroom or beef soup, roast pork or fowl, fish and potatoes, sauerkraut, *koláce*, and dried berries or fruits. Sausages were prepared weeks in advance. Heaps of wild nuts, gathered in the fall, were a traditional part of the holiday feast. Christmas bread was made from dried dough cut into small rounds, which were baked and rolled in honey and poppy seed. The old grandmothers told the girls that if they wanted the boys to like them they must put one of the little biscuits under their pillows at night.

The year following the first appearance of the Christmas tree at the church, many homes adopted the custom. In the old country only people of considerable means had had Christmas trees, and some of the villagers had never heard of them until they came to America. The first home Christmas trees in the Flats were decorated by the children with small homemade cookies, nutshells painted in bright colors, bits of rags or paper, and small candles of twisted wax. Long strings of popcorn and cranberries were also used, in the American fashion.

The custom of exchanging gifts during the Christmas season was not general in old Bohemia, but it was universally adopted in the Flats. The women crocheted square shawls, or fascinators, and made bright sweaters and socks. Boys carved wall plaques from blocks of wood salvaged from the Mississippi. Girls fashioned dolls from straw and rags and finished them off with eyes of bright beads. Families exchanged complete dinners, packing them in split-willow baskets and sending them up the road with the children, who stopped at each house along the way to sing Christmas carols and gather cookies or pennies in return. The church choir also made the rounds of the village, singing carols in front of each home.

Lefse

The potato was a staple of life for most immigrants. Lefse is a pancake-like food cooked on a griddle which incorporates yet another way of cooking this versatile staple. Once served regularly, it has become a Christmas tradition among Scandinavians. Lefse has no leavening agent and thus is very flat as opposed to fluffy latkes, the fried potato pancakes served at Hanukkah.

Take *8 medium-sized potatoes,* boil until tender, and mash (with a fork, food mill, or blender), enough to make 4 cups mashed potatoes. Add *1 tsp. salt, ¼ c. oil* or *shortening, 1 tbsp. sugar,* and *2 tbsp. sweet cream.* Allow this mixture to cool for several hours; this dough should be completely cold. When you are ready to cook add *1-1/3 c. flour* to potatoes and mix. Form ¼ c. dough into a ball and roll out very, very thin on a well-floured board. Bake on a hot grill (400-450 degrees), flipping once as in a pancake when brown dots appear on the underside. Cooks used a special piece of wood, long and flat, and called appropriately enough, a lefse stick, to turn the lefse. Remove from grill after second side is done, fold in half, and cool. These may be stored in refrigerator or freezer. They are not reheated when eaten, but served at room temperature. Spread lightly with *soft butter,* sprinkle with *sugar* or a *cinnamon and sugar* mixture, and roll tightly. TRE

Christmas, Beauty, and Community Service

by Patricia Hampl

Did it begin with Sister Mary Patricia, who taught us Modern European History (which was not modern: the textbook stopped with the end of the Hapsburg Empire, and was itself bound in green watery moiré, a book not only about but from a former time). Sister told us one day that Hans Christian Andersen, the fairytale man, was supposed to have driven through the streets of Prague, hanging lovesick out his carriage window, smitten with the beautiful Czech girls, crying, "Pretty maiden, pretty maiden, let me kiss you!" In passing, Sister mentioned that Bohemian women were considered the most beautiful in Europe. She was a history teacher who could be counted on for this kind of satisfying useless remark.

I raised my hand.

"Yes, Patricia," she said.

I stood up—we had to rise to recite, giving our classrooms a churchy up-and-down quality—and I said, as if in a dream, fatally unconscious, "I'm Bohemian."

Everyone hooted. Even Sister, kindly poker face, smiled and said, "Well, is that so." As I sat down, almost before the room filled with laughter, I came to myself out of that momentary ethnic trance. I couldn't believe I'd actually stood up—braces, pointy glasses, pimples—and said what I'd said.

As a rule, I thought of myself as monumentally ugly. Was I in fact as homely as thought? Impossible. But the mere thought of my looks inflamed my imagination and caused me to see myself as a freak—for no particular reason, simply because I had a physical existence. Like many people obsessed by their appearance, I had no idea what I actually looked like. I was afraid of photographs as if they were evidence brought forward by the prosecution. I studied the mirror solemnly and then, minutes later away from its image, was dismayed to realize I could not remember what the girl in the glass looked like. It was a typical adolescent self-consciousness, but it seemed to last forever. In fact, can I truly say it is finished? Writing about it as an adolescent preoccupation only seems to place it in the past.

I was probably—to use my mother's sane phrase—nice enough looking. My mother was not obsessed by beauty and thought a woman had done her level best if she "put on her face," kept her hair decently combed, and manicured her nails once a week. Perfume, lipstick, nail polish were not, for her, rituals of self-love; they were the spit-and-polish discipline of a good soldier who kept to the forms. She spent no time worrying about the face and body fate had dealt her: they were "nice enough." Beauty was another realm, something that, like inherited wealth, struck rarely—and to other, stranger, beings. Unlike my grandmother and aunts, my mother did not ponder the elusive qualities of beauty, did not ache to be gorgeous—at least, not as far as I knew. Why bother—she looked nice enough. Those who *were* beautiful were, in my mother's cosmology, a joy for the rest of us to behold, not our competition. And in our family it was my father who, everyone agreed, was the beauty. "Handsome as a movie star," my mother's friends would sigh. For a while in first grade I was under the impression that he was president of the United States (he was president of the church Men's Altar Guild that year, I believe). It seemed natural that someone so handsome should run the country.

My father was not only handsome. As a florist he was, to me, somehow in charge of beauty. A man "handsome as a movie star" whose business was beauty. In second grade, when we were given an assignment to find out how our fathers' work "helped the community," I went home with foreboding, sensing that my father's work did not help the community in any way, that in fact it was superfluous to the community. As I saw it, children whose fathers were doctors or house painters, for instance, were home free. But my father's occupation struck me as iffy, lightweight, positively extraneous and therefore (to my Catholic puritan logic) not useful to the community.

I felt this foreboding in spite of the fact that I loved the greenhouse and often played in the palmhouse (which was Africa). I once saw a rabbit give birth to her babies in the root cellar, and in the summer I trailed my finger teasingly across the low pool in the back lot where the goldfish—some of them alarmingly large—and the water plants were kept. In winter I wandered through the moist houses, as each glassy room was called, watching the exotic trick my father played on the Minnesota weather. I read the labels on the huge, ancient rose trees and great geranium plants in expensive pots, which wealthy matrons had left in the greenhouse to be cared for while they went to Florida or Arizona, or, the really ethereal ones, to Italy.

The odor of crushed evergreen, the intense little purple berries of juniper, the fans of cedar and the killing hard work of the Christmas rush *were* Christmas to me. I preferred this marketplace Christmas, full of overworked employees and cross tempers and the endless parade of "gift plants" and boxed cut flowers, to our own family Christmas with its ordinary tree and turkey like everybody else's.

But was any of this of use to the community? Did it do any good? I did not want to put my father on the spot. Still, I had the assignment and I asked my question, beginning first with the innocuous part: what, exactly, was his job? He answered at great and technical length; he loved his work.

Then the real question: "Is your job of any use to the community?" I had decided to word it this way, rather than asking *how* it was useful, sensing as I did that it was of no use whatever. I thought that he could simply say, as painlessly as possible, no. And then we'd just drop the subject. My handsome father, who had been enjoying the interrogation, the opportunity to explain his place in the world, frowned. "What do you mean—is it of any use to the community?" he asked sharply.

"I mean, does it do any good—to the community?" I was flustered and was losing hold of what community meant. I was only eight and the whole thing was beginning to unravel as I saw my movie star father frowning at me.

"Who asked you to ask that?"

"Sister. Sister said," I practically cried, falling back on the Catholic school child's great authority.

"Sister," my father said. He was angry. It was as I had thought: he served no use to the community. He was silent for some time, not weighing his words, but apparently deciding whether to speak at all.

"You tell Sister," he finally said, coldly, as if he were talking to an adult, "I do the most important thing for the community. Do you think people can live without beauty? Flowers—do they kill anybody? Do they hurt anyone? Flowers are beautiful— that's all. That's enough. So they're sending you home to find out what's the *use!* You tell her they're beautiful. Tell her I bring beauty to the community." He said the final word with regal contempt, as if he only used the grimy jargon of Sister and her band of philistines for purposes of argument.

It was less than ten years after the Second World War; the Korean "conflict" was just ended. My father wasn't talking to me, not to an eight-year-old, and probably not to a nun with a "unit on work" in her social studies class. He spoke, I think, to himself, in a cry for values, dismayed that the use of a red rose had to be explained, as if my question were proof that the world had been more brutalized than he had known.

> *St. Paul native Patricia Hampl is an author who has contributed short fiction, essays, and poetry to leading literary publications. Her memoir,* A Romantic Education, *received a Houghton Mifflin Literary Fellowship; her most recent publication is* Spillville.

Christmas Eve in the City
by Oliver Towne

Along about 4:30 p.m. the lights begin to come on and a strange quiet muffles the city with the dusk.

And if you go up one of the seven hills of St. Paul and watch and listen, you feel the stillness of the city below on Christmas eve. Even in the chilly wind the warmth of this one night will rise off the forests of buildings.

In the now dim, almost empty aisles of the department stores on Wabasha and Robert, the fever of the weeks before has subsided. The white covers have been drawn over the confusion of the counters. Only the echoes of the shoppers' frenzy, the employees' parties at the end still ring faintly.

The people have long ago left the loop. In place of the 5 p.m. rush hour, the last trickle of the stream of humanity rides out on buses and cars, leaving only rows of parking meters like picket fences. The Minnesota Mutual chimes play to an empty house at 5 p.m.

There are gay, bright lights in the city tonight, but not from the flashing neon of the cafes and bars, night clubs or taverns. These, too, are dark. For tonight the lights belong to Christmas—to the lighted trees, shining out of mansion and hovel alike. Of decorations swinging in the night wind, spotlights bathing church steeples, which point like beacons into the darkness.

There is music in the city, too. For this night—at least—it is not rock'n'roll or the discordant jangle of the music of an era or a generation. It is the music of the ages, rising in a crescendo from an organ in a church, from voices gathered around a piano, playing out of the radio in the cab that prowls the streets, on the desk of the hotel night clerk.

It is the tune that the patrolman hums to himself as he walks his beat along Jackson street and the nun recalls from her childhood as she keeps her vigil in the corridors of St. Joseph's hospital. And the soft caroling down the halls of Ancker hospital drowns out the cries of anguish in the receiving room and the moan of the siren at the back door.

You hear it, too, reverberating through the vaulted Union depot concourse, played by the organ set in the center, a perfect background for the happy shouts of friends and families in arm-in-arm reunion at Gate 11 or 12 or 18. And down in the trainshed, in the half light of the limited's locomotive cab, the engineer opens his lunchbox and takes out a cold sandwich and whistles a Christmas tune as he recalls Christmas eves of his boyhood.

And I wonder if the pilot of the plane, winging across the city for a landing, imagines himself as something like a Santa Claus, bringing human gifts to people waiting in the terminal? Or does he sing "Jingle Bells" to himself?

And so you stand there on one of the seven hills of St. Paul and look across it on Christmas eve. Then you think how it is with some of the people hidden behind those lights.

There's Casey, the cab driver, taking people to midnight church services, and you know he won't have to spend Christmas in his lonely room. You wonder which of the many invitations to dinner he accepted—those that were phoned in to you.

You remember another lonely man. Father George Skluzacek, chaplain at the Carmelite convent at Lake Demontreville, and remember the care with which the Guild of Catholic Women packed his gifts while you watched a week ago. "He is one of our special people," they said.

For just a minute you think about Mrs. Gladys Weins, alone tonight at 1641 S. Concord, who took her widow's mite and turned it into Christmas cards for hundreds of men and women in prisons. And you remember the story you heard yesterday about Wilhelm Raade, Norwegian seafarer and artist, who brought his wife and 16-year-old daughter to the city and about the hopes he has that this will be the promised city for a 61-year-old artist, yet the dwindling cash in his pocket was not enough to buy them much of a Christmas for their little apartment. So their only friend in the city, a guy named Al Smith, took what little he had and gave it to them.

You'd like to look in, too, on the bare apartments and tattered houses and see the looks on the faces of all the children who will know Christmas is for them, too, because of the generosity of the city. A lot of those lights out there tonight are halos being worn.

You have a thought, too, for a little girl named Shannon Neagle, who was 9 and didn't quite live to see the city tonight. Her funeral was yesterday. But the gift she left is as wonderful as any that will be given this year. Her illness created a bond of friendship among the families who live in Windward Heights No. 2. They learned the joy of unselfishness.

Suddenly, standing there on the hill, you know that word the key to the way it is in the city tonight.

It is mirrored in the judge who will forsake his own Christmas dinner tomorrow to eat with the prisoners in the City Workhouse and talk with each of them.

It is the stranger you meet on the street corner tonight, who wishes you a "Merry Christmas" instead of passing without recognition. The cop who buys the transient a cup of coffee and finds him a bed at the Union Gospel Mission.

And so you walk back into the city, with only one regret. That it is like this in the city only once a year.

A car passes and the driver leans out and shouts:

"Merry Christmas!"

"Merry Christmas!" you shout back. And it's meant for everybody.

Coming Home

by F. Scott Fitzgerald

One of my most vivid memories is of coming back West from prep school and later from college at Christmas time. Those who went farther than Chicago would gather in the old dim Union Station at six o'clock of a December evening, with a few Chicago friends, already caught up into their own holiday gayeties, to bid them a hasty good-by. I remember the fur coats of the girls returning from Miss This-or-That's and the chatter of frozen breath and the hands waving overhead as we caught sight of old acquaintances, and the matchings of invitations: "Are you going to the Ordways'? the Herseys'? the Schultzes'?" and the long green tickets clasped tight in our gloved hands. And last the murky yellow cars of the Chicago, Milwaukee & St. Paul railroad looking cheerful as Christmas itself on the tracks beside the gate.

When we pulled out into the winter night and the real snow, our snow, began to stretch out beside us and twinkle against the windows, and the dim lights of small Wisconsin stations moved by, a sharp wild brace came suddenly into the air. We drew in deep breaths of it as we walked back from dinner through the cold vestibules, unutterably aware of our identity with this country for one strange hour, before we melted indistinguishably into it again.

That's my Middle West—not the wheat or the prairies or the lost Swede towns, but the thrilling returning trains of my youth, and the street lamps and sleigh bells in the frosty dark and the shadows of holly wreaths thrown by lighted windows on the snow. I am part of that, a little solemn with the feel of those long winters . . .

Dodger's Christmas

by Jon Hassler

Boys with records of good behavior and homes to go to were released from the Home School for 10 days at Christmas. Dodger Hicks was one of them. On the afternoon of Christmas Eve, two days after the other boys had left, he stood on the porch of the main building and watched for Mr. Cranshaw's car to turn in at the gate. In a cardboard box at his feet were a change of underwear and socks, a clean shirt, and several comic books. It was Mr. Cranshaw, his Winona County case worker, who had delivered Dodger to the Flensboro Home School for Boys in October. He was a sharp-faced little man with a brusque manner and not much to say, but with a certain amount of compassion in his eyes. Dodger had been grateful when, after his sentencing for robbery, Mr. Cranshaw assured the judge and the sheriff that Dodger did not require an armed guard on his way to Flensboro, 60 miles upriver from Winona.

The clouds of Christmas Eve were darkening to gunmetal blue and threatening to unload a heavy snowfall into the Mississippi Valley. Dodger wore no cap; his bald head was numb with cold. His jacket was a thin flannel shirt he had appropriated for himself in the laundry room, where he had been working half days since being declared uneducable by the teaching staff. On his feet were warm, sturdy work boots lent him by the barber who came out from Flensboro every second Thursday and shaved 109 heads. "Are those raggedy old things the only shoes you've got?" the barber asked him. "You can't go home for Christmas looking like a bum."

The barber, whose name was Johnson, took a special interest in Dodger, more than once having spoken to the warden about the two cigarette burns near Dodger's hairline that were slow to heal. Dodger admitted to Mr. Johnson that they were caused by older boys poking him with lighted cigarettes after he fell asleep at night, but he didn't tell him of the several other scars on his arms and back. The warden finally relented and allowed Dodger to see the doctor during his weekly visit to the school. The doctor gave Dodger a tube of ointment for his burns and he gave the warden a piece of his mind for allowing physical abuse in the dormitories. "If you don't take action," the doctor threatened. "I'll report it to the governor and the state board of health." The warden's only action was to warn Johnson to quit meddling in the affairs of the Home School or else lose his barbering contract with the state.

In an office at the front of the main building, the warden looked up from his desk and saw Cranshaw's car turn in at the gate. He clapped a hat on his head and scurried out to the porch. "Come on, Hicks, we can't keep your man waiting." The warden despised Dodger for not being mean and tough. Most boys Dodger's age— 15—quickly learned how to fight back and defend themselves in the Home School, but Dodger never got over being agreeable, as if he expected everybody else to be as dreamy and soft-hearted as himself.

Dodger picked up his box and descended the steps with the warden. One of the few things Dodger had in common with the other boys was his dislike of the warden, whose eyes were icy and whose mustache and pointed goatee reminded Dodger of drawings he had seen of the devil. He went around the car and got in on the passenger side while Mr. Cranshaw rolled down his window and greeted the warden.

"About time you got here," piped the warden.

"I told you I was tied up till today." Mr. Cranshaw handed him a document.

"It wasn't in our budget to feed the kid for two extra days. How come his mother didn't come for him?"

"She has no car."

The warden glanced at the signatures at the bottom of the document and said, "All right, take him away, and be sure he's back here by suppertime on New Year's Day. And while you're at it, give him a talking to about laziness. He makes no effort in his classes and he makes no effort in the laundry. He's well on his way to being a derelict."

Mr. Cranshaw rolled his window shut before the warden finished. He shifted gears, and the car moved down the sloping drive.

"Well, how have you been, Dodger?"

"Not so bad," Dodger smiled. He sat holding his box on his lap.

"You sound like you've got a cold."

"Yeah. It's real hot in the laundry, and then I go outside and my nose runs."

"Haven't you got a cap? You'll freeze your head."

"Yeah, I've got a cap but I keep forgetting it. It's hard to keep wearing a cap when you never did."

Driving out through the gate, Cranshaw felt a sense of freedom almost as great as Dodger's. Over the years he had seen enough of the Home School to detest it. His work took him to prisons, hospitals, orphanages, insane asylums and schools for the blind and deaf, none of which made his skin crawl the way this institution did. The guards were thugs and the warden was a martinet with a treacherous look in his eye.

"Dodger, your mother isn't home. I called her last week to make sure she'd sign your release form. She said she'd sign it, but when I went to the apartment this morning the landlady said she's been gone a week or more. But she expects her home for Christmas."

Dodger shrugged and nodded and shrugged again.

"I'm not supposed to take you home, Dodger without your mother being there."

Dodger said nothing.

"But I'm taking you anyhow. I forged your mother's name."

Dodger chuckled.

They rode on in silence. The highway was a narrow winding shelf at the base of the bluffs. Below them the blue-black river was dotted with small ice floes. It was dark when they reached Winona. Snow was dropping in large, watery flakes. Cranshaw drew up in front of a house facing the highway and said, "OK, Dodger, I'm sticking my neck out for you, so return the favor by staying out of trouble, will you?"

"Sure."

"Your landlady said to tell you she wouldn't be home tonight but she's left your apartment unlocked. I'll pick you up on New Year's afternoon."

"OK."

"Merry Christmas, Dodger." He gave him a five-dollar bill.

"Merry Christmas."

Snowflakes melted and ran down the dome of his scalp as Dodger carried his box into the tiny front hallway and climbed the stairs.

He wished the landlady, Mrs. Wrobleski, were home. She had been nice to him during the short time he lived here before the robbery, offering him a cookie or a cupcake every so often. He opened the door at the head of the stairs and entered the apartment. He switched on the light. His mother's bed in the living room was unmade. Standing on the table and the two windowsills were a number of empty beer bottles. He went into the kitchen and saw that his mother had been using his cot as a catch-all for clothes and groceries. He added his cardboard box to the clutter on the cot and went to the refrigerator for something to drink. He uncapped a bottle of milk and took a big swallow before he realized it was sour. He went into the tiny bathroom, spat into the sink and drank a glass of water.

He returned to the living room and pulled a chair up to the window. He watched the headlights moving along the highway below him. He savored his solitude. After two months in the Home School, this was pure peace. There was no one to taunt him or hurt him or put him to work. He was glad his mother was gone. Ever since his father was sent to prison for embezzlement, Christmases were hard on his mother. She drank and got weepy, then drank some more and got angry, and then drank some more and slept. With his father present, come to think of it, her behavior wasn't all that much different, except the weepy part was shorter and the angry part was longer. "For them that can be merry," she'd say when anyone wished her "Merry Christmas." Wherever she was tonight, Dodger hoped she was with a man she liked, someone thoughtful enough to give her a present.

It dawned on Dodger that he had no present for her. He went to the closet and found a cap he hadn't seen before, a black watch cap probably left behind by a riverboat man. He pulled the cap down over his ears and left the house. Snow slanted into his face as he hurried along the highway toward the lighted sign of the Conoco station. He feared it might close early because it was Christmas Eve, but he got there in time. He stopped in the shadows beyond the gas pumps and saw only one attendant on duty, luckily not the same man who had caught him stealing money from the till. The attendant was giving change to the driver of a pickup, and there were two cars waiting for service. Dodger unbuttoned the cuffs of his flannel shirt, then went up to the man and asked if he could use the toilet. The man said sure.

Dodger went into the grimy, brightly lit station and looked around, making his choices, his heart beating wildly as it always did in the act of stealing. Keeping his eye on the man pumping gas, he slipped a Zippo lighter into the pocket of his flannel shirt and a candy bar up his left sleeve. He went into the restroom while the attendant came in and rang up a sale and went out again. He emerged from the restroom and studied a standing display of windshield-wiper blades. He put a blade up his right sleeve and opened the door and left, the thrill of success washing over him, his heart beating faster and faster. Stealing was wrong, he knew, and most people were dead-set against it, but how could you resist doing the one thing in life you were good at?

He walked through the deepening snow, buttoning his shirt cuffs and taking pleasure in the warmth of his feet in the barber's thick-soled boots. He walked to the neighborhood store where his mother bought groceries. A bell tinkled over the door as he opened it. The old woman proprietor came out from her sitting room at the back and said "Merry Christmas" before she saw who it was. She replaced her smile with a stony glare. He saw at once that there would be no stealing from this woman. He bought a bottle of pop, a sack of potato chips and a tin of shoe polish the color of the barber's boots.

He went home and put the Zippo, his mother's gift, on the dresser. When Mrs. Wrobleski came home he would ask her for a scrap of wrapping paper. As he ate his candy bar and drank his pop, he examined the windshield-wiper blade, disappointed in himself for having stolen it simply because it was available. He had no use for it. It was Dodger's policy to steal only out of necessity and never—or seldom—at random.

When he finished eating he put the wiper blade in his cardboard box and took out a clean handkerchief. He opened the tin of shoe polish and went to work on Mr. Johnson's boots, applying three coats of polish and buffing them with his handkerchief. When he finished they gleamed like new. He resolved to pick up a new pair of bootlaces before he returned them to Mr. Johnson.

Then he sat by the window and watched the Christmas Eve traffic diminish to almost nothing. Snow fell thickly, like feathers, and he grew very sleepy watching it. He moved to his mother's bed and fell immediately into a deep sleep. Sometime after midnight he awoke with a cry, having dreamed that he was about to be burned with a cigarette. He lay with his eyes open for a minute, savoring the stillness and peace of the empty house; then he turned over and went back to sleep.

A leading Minnesota writer of fiction, Jon Hassler's books include Staggerford, Simon's Night, Jemmy, The Love Hunter, A Green Journey, *and* Grand Opening. *He has won a Book-of-the-Year Award from Friends of American Writers and fellowships from the Guggenheim Foundation and the Minnesota State Arts Board. He currently teaches at St. John's University in Central Minnesota.*

The Flight into Egypt

CELEBRATING
THE NATIVITY

Christmas in a New Land

by Vilhem Moberg

Yuletide was near—a strange Yule for Kristina, a Christmas in another world, a Christmas without Yule chores. No pig to butcher, no ale to brew, no great-bake to bake. But they must nevertheless celebrate the holiday and honor the Saviour's birth like Christian people. She said to Karl Oskar, this year they must not think of the outside—food, drink, and material things. They must celebrate Christmas in their hearts; this year must be a Christmas for their souls.

She scoured the cabin floor until it was shining white, she washed their underclothes in ash lye, so that all could change for the holiday, she hung fresh pine boughs on the walls and decked the cabin inside as best she could. Of a pine top with upright branches Karl Oskar made a five-armed candlestick, an ingenuity which his wife praised greatly. He had promised they would celebrate Christmas at a table, and he kept his promise: on Christmas Eve itself he gave the table the last finishing touches with his plane. He was proud of his handicraft, the first piece of real furniture he had ever made, particularly when, at the final inspection, Kristina said: This sturdy oak table would undoubtedly last so long that not only they themselves but their children and grandchildren as well could eat their meals at it throughout their whole lives.

While they had eaten their meals at the chest lid Karl Oskar had felt like a pauper sitting in a corner of someone else's house, eating handed-out food. Now, as he put his feet under his own table, his self-confidence increased: Now he had settled down, now he had become his own master in the new land.

They used their new table for the first time at the Christmas Eve dinner. And Kristina too was pleased—to gather for a feast around a table was something quite different from sitting down to a meal at the old chest lid. The five-armed candleholder was put in the center of the table; they had saved only three candles for Christmas, so two arms were left empty, but the three burning candles spread Yule light in their house. They had bought a pound of rice for the Christmas porridge, and with it they used sweet milk. It was their only Christmas dish, but they ate it with a deep sense of holiday spirit. Its smell and taste brought to their mind recollections of this Holy Eve's celebration at home. Long-ago Christmases now entered their cabin, Christmas Eves with the whole family gathered; and their thoughts lingered on those who at other Yuletides had sat down at table with them. Relatives at home in Sweden tonight seemed more alive than ever, and they spoke of the letter from Sweden which they had been waiting for so long. How much longer before they would hear from parents and relatives? The expected mail from Sweden had not had time to arrive before the river froze and the packets stopped coming for the winter. Now it could not arrive until spring, and that was a long time to wait.

Tonight Karl Oskar remembered his parents as he had seen them that last morning—when he had looked back from the wagon seat for a final glimpse of them as he left the old home: father and mother, looking after the departing ones, standing on the stoop close together, immobile as two statues. To him they would always remain in that position; they could not move or walk away; they stood there, looking after their departing sons; they stood like two dead objects, hewn in stone. His parents could never again resume life in his mind's eye. Perhaps this was because deep within him he knew he would never again meet them on this earth.

A thought came to him—it remained a thought only, which he would not utter: his father and mother might already be dead and buried, without his knowledge. . . .

After the meal Kristina opened the Bible and read the second chapter from St. Luke which in her home had always been read by her father on Christmas Eve in commemoration of the Saviour's birth:

"And so it was, that, while they were there, the days were accomplished that she should be delivered.

"And she brought forth her first-born son, and wrapped him in swaddling clothes, and laid him in a manger; because there was no room for them in the inn. . . ."

Kristina read the Christmas Gospel for all of them, but after a few verses she felt as though she were reading it for herself only: it concerned her above all, it concerned her more than the listeners. Mary's delivery in the stable in Bethlehem reminded her of the childbed she had but recently gone through. It seemed that Mary's time too had come suddenly and unprepared for, even though her days were accomplished: Mary had been on a journey, and perhaps they had been delayed, unable to reach home in time. And Mary had been poor, even more impoverished than she herself. Kristina had borne her child in a human abode, in a well-timbered house—Mary had lain on straw in an animal shelter, in a stall. Kristina enjoyed the comfort of a kind and helpful midwife, but the Bible said not one word about any help-woman for Mary in the stable. And she wondered whence the Saviour's mother had obtained the swaddling clothes she wrapped about her child before she placed it in the manger. Had she prepared them in advance and brought them along on the journey to Bethlehem? The Bible was so sparing with details that she often wondered and questioned while reading. She guessed Mary must have had as much concern about the clothing of her first born as she herself had had for her child. Perhaps Mary too had been forced to cut up her petticoat to prepare the swaddling clothes for Jesus.

For the first time in twenty years Kristina slept on Christmas morning; ever since early childhood she had gone with her parents on this morning to the early service, which took place hours before daylight, the church illuminated with many candles. But here also they would revere Christmas Day, and Second Christmas Day: all work in the house ceased. They carried in enough firewood before the holiday, all they had to do was to tend the fire and prepare food.

". . . we have had a happy Christmas and a Christmas-tree party for the children, I mean the schoolchildren. Here it is beginning to get like Sweden, at least at Christmastime, for there is both lutefisk and Christmas porridge, besides a lot of other good things, but the latter are more everyday things . . ."

Letter of Carl and Fred Bergman
January 23, 1896

❧ ❧ ❧

Topics of conversation in the evenings covered everything possible but as Christmas drew near, they began to concentrate more and more on memories from Sweden. When Christmas Eve came and we had eaten our supper a kind of pious feeling lay in the air. There was not the noise and merriment that were otherwise so typical of our evenings. Many sat by themselves dreaming. The standing rule, "lights out" at nine o'clock, did not apply that night, and when nine o'clock had passed one of our accordion virtuosos started to play melodies from the homeland and it did not take long before there was a thunder of Swedish singing in our cabin which continued with only short pauses until Christmas morning had come. When it was already a good bit into Christmas morning, our bosun began "Var halsad skona morgonstund" with a voice many ministers would have envied him for, and we joined in as best we could, and a little better.

Next day around eight we were up and about before breakfast and Christmas Day was just like any other day except that the cook added a few extras to the food. The day after, the bookkeeper came with the timber drivers and had with him the company's mail pouch, and I daresay that never was Saint Nicholas more heartily received than our bookkeeper when he came with the mailbag.

A Lake-of-the-Woods lumbercamp, 1913

Julgrat - Swedish Christmas Pudding

Rice pudding was frequently mentioned in recipe books of the nineteenth century. It was boiled, then steamed over water, a feat which could be accomplished over an open fire or primitive stove. Scandinavians, especially the Swedish, served this dish on Christmas Eve with an almond hidden inside, the almond being a token of good luck in the New Year for the one finding it.

To prepare, first soften the rice. Measure *1 c. rice.* Wash and drain it, then add to *2 qts. boiling water.* Bring to a boil again, and cool uncovered for 1 minute. Drain the water thoroughly and add *2 tbsp. butter.* Put rice, *1 tsp. salt, 3 tbsp. sugar,* and *5 c. milk* in top of double boiler. Cover and cook gently over boiling water until rice is tender and milk is absorbed, about 2 hours. Stir *1 blanched whole almond* into rice. Spoon into bowls and serve warm, with *cream,* sprinkled with *cinnamon* and *sugar* on top.

TRE

Singing Latin in New Ulm

by Bill Holm

When north Europe's cast-offs moved to Minnesota, they left some baggage behind. The Germans didn't move Goethe, or the Poles Chopin; the Danes forgot Holberg, and the Swedes did not invite Strindberg to join them here. But they brought both their religions with new ferocity in them further from the sea, and the rudiments of their old country church architecture. In western Minnesota brick is Catholic, wood is Lutheran. Tiny bare frame churches contain Norwegians or Icelanders, but anything with a dome, spires, ornamental glass, and stone is likely to be full of Poles or Germans. Thus New Ulm, like its European namesake, is a cathedral town.

On a sunny Sunday afternoon in mid-winter, the Prairie Chorale sings its Christmas concert in that old cathedral. Harsh light goldens the stone, brightening up dim corners in the big vaulted room. Like all stone interiors, this is full of echos that magnify the smallest sound many times beyond itself. As the audience grows, there rises a steady buzz of shuffling overshoes, scratching wool, squishing goose-down, muffled whispering that's like an undertone of oversized out-of-season crickets. Medieval cathedrals must have been like this too—never silent, a single sneeze resounding like a gunshot or a helicopter rising.

The singers process; the buzz diminuendos; two hundred folded programs do not open simultaneously. The concert opens with a Pachelbel *Magnificat*.

> *Magnificat anima mea Dominum.*
> *Et exultavit spiritus meus in Deo salutari meo.*

The counterpoint threads onward toward the phrase that ended almost everything sung or said inside churches like this for thousands of years:

> *Gloria Patri, et Filio, Et Spiritui Sancto.*
> *Sicut erat in principio, et nunc, et semper,*
> *et in saecula saeculorum, Amen.*

The Chorale performs decently. Singing in a stone bowl clearly delights them, and they stand listening for ten seconds after the piece to the ghost of their own voices saying *Amen* all over the room. Under it, as everyone there understands whether conscious of it or not, is the ghost of that *Gloria* in Chartres, Cologne, York Minster, Norwegian stave churches, St. Peter's and St. Paul's, and old Ulm itself. The ghost of Europe, uncomfortable in this midwest winter light, does its best to remain beautiful and intelligent.

The singers peer out over a lake of faces swimming in the ancient noise of that music. The front row is most beautiful: a line of old priests, white hair rising over white collars, pink wrinkles between, suits black as whale bodies. Not one of those priests seems likely to see eighty again, and you imagine them alive at the foundation of the world, black and white and ancient even then. They weep while they smile! The mightiest weeping of all comes from the chief priest sitting on the aisle.

After some Christmas carols, the director turns and announces to the audience that four *Ave Marias* will be sung, and that it is appropriate to do this since today is the Feast of the Immaculate Conception. Ancestors of almost everyone in the room were persecuted or killed depending on whether or not they entertained this particular theological idea, but the young blond director does not mention this, nor should he. This is Minnesota, an afternoon for rejoicing of heart.

Four *Aves* come: an ancient plain song; austere counterpoint form the Renaissance; a romantic Russian setting; finally, a dissonant one composed by an American. Four times those words return, always the same, whatever the notes that embroider them.

> *Ave Maria, gratia plena,*
> *Dominus tecum.*
> *Benedicta tu in mulieribus,*
> *Et benedictus fructus ventris tui, Jesus.*
> *Sancta Maria, Mater Dei,*
> *Ora pro nobis peccatoribus,*
> *Nunc et in hora mortis nostrae.*

The joyful weeping from the old priests, huge tears of praise streaming down the wrinkled creek beds on their cheeks, now overwhelms the singers too, and the afternoon continues as if magically presided over by the Virgin herself who heard her name called four times and appeared as an invisible presence under the stone vaulting. The music now sounds that forgiveness often spoken about in rooms like this. Something female softens the prairies today, maybe even, for one afternoon, America.

At the end of the concert, more Latin, perhaps the greatest sentence of all:

> *O magnum mysterium,*
> *et admirable sacramentum,*
> *Ut animalia viderent Dominum natum . . .*

What a great mystery that animals should see a God born! And yet, who else would notice it? Men, busy with practical missiles and fertilizers have to be worked on by magic before they stop their quarrels long enough to watch and listen with any openness of heart or intelligence.

"Silent Night" in German with a guitar, and then the singers recess to the basement to smoke, compliment each other, get into street clothes, and drive on to another concert. Magic cannot last too long or it loses power; Beethoven broke the spell cast by his dreamy improvisations with harsh banged chords.

But it continues a little while. The singers stop buzzing suddenly; a presence enters the basement, the beautiful old chief priest who sat on the aisle staunches his tears while hugging the director. He speaks:

"I was bishop of this diocese for 30 years, have been in this cathedral church my whole life as a priest, and I have never heard anything so beautiful as the great gift of music you gave this afternoon. And your Latin! It is so wonderful to hear Latin again after all these years; and you sing it so clearly, so correctly with such feeling, and . . ." he pauses, and a sad shadow passes over his moist face, "I suppose . . ." he is almost choking, "you are all," another burst of tears, "Protestants."

Prostestants! Indeed they are. O magnum mysterium. . . .

Bill Holm, a native of Minneota, Minnesota is a poet and scholar of Icelandic extraction. He was a Fulbright lecturer in American Literature at the University of Iceland at Reykjavick, and has been the recipient of awards and critical acclaim for both poetry and prose. Books by Holm include Boxelder Bug Variations *and* Prairie Days.

A Festival of Lessons and Carols

by Sister Owen Lindblad

The Festival began a century or more ago in Cornwall, England at the Truro Cathedral. Its songs and scriptural lessons soon became a traditional hailing of the Savior's Birth, and were presented each Christmas Eve at King's College in Cambridge, England.

Far from English shores, in the small Church of the Good Samaritan in Sauk Centre, Minnesota, the old custom found new enthusiasts. In 1964, the first Festival was presented under the direction of Dr. J.C. Grant. The program was modified and adapted to the tiny Episcopal Church build here in 1867, itself more than a century old.

Christmas, 1987, marks the 21st performance of the Festival of Lessons and Carols. Dr. Grant no longer accompanies the choir on the majestic pipe organ which he himself built back in the 1950s. Since his death in 1984, others have sat at the keyboard. But the rich, deep tones of over 1,245 pipes continue to resound and give new life to the age-old Christmas story.

You must arrive early. As you take your seat in the small Gothic style church, you are suddenly transported to an earlier era, to an English countryside chapel. Around you, at each window, candles glow pensively. Green garlands and wreaths and red pointsettias complete the simplicity of the little church's decor. You glance at the program, at the lesson of preparation for Christ's Birth beginning with Genesis, the prophesies of Isaias, the New Testament revelation to Mary, and finally the unfolding of the Wonderful Birth.

The silence of the sacred milieu is broken as the 60-member choir enters, garbed in crimson and gold, bursting forth in song with "Once in Royal David's City." You are plunged at once into the setting for the magnificent Mystery of the Incarnation.

After the ancient carols and seven lessons have been proclaimed, you are amazed to be there, to be at the lowly manger in Bethlehem, joining in the tender refrains of Franz Gruber's beloved "Silent Night." You are reluctant to leave. But Christmas is here and the joy and wonder at so great an event once again penetrates the modern, midwestern world. You take the gift out gratefully into the frosty night.

Saint Sulpice

by Carol Bly

Once I was lost in Paris. I had got away from the Seine, on the Left Bank, and eventually came to the Place de Saint Sulpice, named for the church in its center. All round the square were small and large shops selling devotional statuary—not hundreds but thousands of plasticine Virgins and Josephs and Marys, donkeys visiting Christ, the sheep and the Wise Men, shepherds. Those I handled were white, ready to be painted by the buyer or perhaps to be left white for the effect of purity. I saw little attempt by the sculptors to *start where the people are*—that convincing approach of grantsmen and teachers.

These figures started, rather, in some dreamhouse of Western religions. Animals, men, son of God—all were refined, all pure white; the people had the high foreheads of Norman and Breton Frenchmen. There was no nonense about the Wise Men having had to ride camels or sleep several nights in these robes. These camels did not bite, and unlike Eliot's, were not refractory. As I looked at the thousands of figures (for there were several shop windows full of them), I realized that the villages the Wise Men passed through were full of latent theologians, and apparently we who buy figures for our crèches are latent theologians, too—even those of us who buy the worst offenders, the tiny Veronicas with bloody veils and the youths who look like Shattuck boys with daubs of red spots on palms and feet, or the Virgins for some reason placed in tiny Coldstream sentry boxes. Parisians call all such devotional crockery *saint sulpice,* since so much of it is sold around that church.

What is the good of *saint sulpice*? The good of it is that whoever thought up the idea of a crèche at all, who was likely St. Francis of Assisi, had heart to know that *starting where the people are* is at best useless. What we all care for is what we yearn to be—not what or where we seem to be. Any art, even *saint sulpice,* that reminds us of what we yearn to be is a help.

Essayist and lecturer Carol Bly is the author of a highly acclaimed book of essays, Letters from the Country, *and* Backbone, *a short story collection. She teaches writing at Hamline University in St. Paul, Minnesota, and is a radio commentator on the literary scene.*

Christmas Morning

by Elizabeth Madox Roberts

If Bethlehem were here today,
Or this were very long ago,
There wouldn't be a winter time
Nor any cold or snow.

I'd run out through the garden gate,
And down along the pasture walk;
And off beside the cattle barns
I'd hear a kind of gentle talk.

I'd move the heavy iron chain
And pull away the wooden pin;
I'd push the door a little bit
And tiptoe very softly in.

The pigeons and the yellow hens
And all the cows would stand away;
Their eyes would open wide to see
A lady in the manger hay,

If this were very long ago
And Bethlehem were here today.

And Mother held my hand and smiled—
I mean the lady would—and she
Would take the woolly blankets off
Her little boy so I could see.

His shut-up eyes would be asleep,
And he would look like our John,
And he would be all crumpled too,
And have a pinkish color on.

I'd watch his breath go in and out.
His little clothes would all be white.
I'd slip my finger in his hand
To feel how he could hold it tight.

And she would smile and say, "Take care,"
The mother, Mary, would, "Take care";
And I would kiss his little hand
And touch his hair.

While Mary put the blankets back
The gentle talk would soon begin.
And when I'd tiptoe softly out
I'd meet the wise men going in.

A Christmas Homily

by Bishop Jerome Hanus, O.S.B.

Bishop Jerome Hanus, O.S.B., ordained and installed as Bishop of St. Cloud on August 24, 1987, delivered the following Christmas Homily, at St. Mary's Cathedral in St. Cloud, Minn., on December 25, 1987.

On this Christmas night, dearly beloved in the Lord, our hearts and minds are drawn to Bethlehem. According to the Gospel, when the shepherds arrived in Bethlehem, they found there Mary and Joseph and the baby lying in the manger. I would invite you to reflect with me a moment about each of these three individuals who made up that first Christmas.

Of course, the most important person is the child Jesus. We know from our faith that this is not an ordinary child like any other child. This is the Son of God, the One who came to save the world from the darkness of sin and death. Nevertheless this looks like an ordinary infant, this child Jesus. He is as helpless as any newborn child. He needs to be taken care of, to be wrapped up, to be nursed, to be kept warm. The human infant is that kind of a being, totally helpless. And it remains for quite some time one of the most totally dependent things you can imagine.

Why do I mention that? Not to remind you of the details of human biology but to make a point about our faith. The helplessness of the child indicates to what limits God will go in the desire to associate with us completely. Christ did not think being God was something to be clung to. He emptied himself completely of his divine prerogatives and took on the form of a slave. He became one of us and shared in our human condition at its weakest point, infancy, so that he could understand us and feel with us and in the end suffer with us. It was in this way that God became one of us. All to what purpose? That we might be saved.

But the child is not alone. The child is surrounded by two other individuals. There is first of all Mary his mother. We think very highly of her. She is the Virgin Mary, the object of God's special concern and love. She has been the subject of innumerable works of art and the topic of much religious thought and poetry and she will always remain a figure of deep affection and inspiration. This evening, however, without any intention of slighting her, I would like to spend a little more time on the third figure present at that first Christmas, the figure of Joseph.

I think we tend to ignore him. But in many ways he stands there as a symbol for us. If we reflect on it a bit, I think that we can identify with him more easily than with the other two. But let me first share with you a little story about Joseph that I heard recently.

A certain teacher was working in a parish religious education program and trying especially hard to help her first graders understand the story of Christmas and to understand that the central fact was the birth of Christ. She was trying to help her children to pay less attention to Santa Claus and all the commercialism connected with this season. So the teacher read the Gospel story to them several times. She taught them to sing "Silent Night" and even produced a little show, a one-act play recreating that first Christmas. Finally she asked them all to make their own Christmas cards depicting the birth of Christ. One youngster created an especially good card. He had drawn the baby in the manger, two adults, and the rest of the features of the scene. But the teacher noticed that the Joseph figure was very large and very fat. And she suspected that this child was trying to sneak Santa Claus back into the scene so she questioned him. "Bobby, who is that? You're not trying to get Santa Claus in your card." The child answered her in all innocence, "Oh, teacher, that is John." "Who's John?" the teacher countered. And the student replied, "Well, you know, the fat fellow we sing about in 'Silent Night.' It's round John Virgin."

That's a child's attempt to understand—probably misunderstand—Joseph. But I'd like to look at Joseph now, as I mentioned, from the eyes of an adult and to think of how he must have experienced the event of Christmas. After all, according to the culture of his day, he was the head of his family and he was the one responsible to see that all matters of importance were taken care of. It was his responsibility to comply with the laws of the state regarding the Roman census. He was the one who had to provide for the well-being of his young wife. He had to find a place for them to spend the night. But in fact in all these responsibilities he proved quite ineffective, quite powerless.

But that's looking at things only on the external side. The same was even more true when you consider what he must have been thinking and feeling on the inside this first Christmas. After all, he was worrying about a woman and her child knowing all the time that this child was not his. He had to act as if he had full responsibility for this situation but in fact a power much greater than his own had intervened. So could we blame him if he were perplexed? Wouldn't it be understandable if he felt confused even lost in the face of these happenings which were really beyond his control?

But that is why I think that he can stand as a symbol for you and me and for most people of our day. We often like to think that we are in complete control of our situations. We think that we can shape events according to our hopes and desires and we think that we can implement our plans and realize our projects if we just put our minds and our shoulders to them. We think that we can create a better world, a world in which peace will prevail, in which suffering will be eliminated, in which injustice will be alleviated, in which prejudice, hatred, and torture will be eliminated. We like to think that if we are upright, good people we can get all this done—if we just work at it hard enough. But Joseph, too, was an upright and just man. He knew what he had to do and he had the will to do it. But could he save the situation? Could he control it? Not in any way.

So also our human nature by itself falls short, far short of its desires. You and I need to be saved. Though we dream of a world and a society of peace and justice, we know only too well from our experience, our experience of ourselves as well as of others, that we are sinners. We know that we fall far short of the glory which God intends for us.

So, my friends, it is very true that we can be saved only by God. But God has loved us so much that we came into the weakness of our situation. We are redeemed by the God who shared our sense of helplessness, by the One who became as dependent as any human infant is. We are saved of our sins because Jesus the Christ brought the love and the mercy of God to our human condition. Joseph standing there in that first Christmas in all his powerlessness, needy, not controlling, reminds us of our need.

This is my first Christmas in Minnesota and my first as bishop. I want to thank you for your welcome and your support, and I want you to know that you are in my thoughts and my prayers today and every day. May Christ bring warmth, light, and renewed life to us all. May peace fill our hearts, our lives, and our world. ✝✝✝

To each and every one of our readers, on the eve of this the best of all the year's holidays, we wish a Merry Christmas! May each one have a light heart, a good conscience, a well filled pocket and a big dinner. May the little ones find their stockings overflowing with the treasures brought by good old Santa Claus from his wondrous far-off treasure cave, the revelling among whose mysteries is the crowning delight of childhood's imagination. May they have all the good things their hearts desire.

But in all our Christmas festivities remember the poor, whom "ye have always with you." Spare from your overburdened board a portion for those whom fate has favored with but the scanty necessaries of life, on whom misfortune has weighed down into actual suffering. Let their necessities be with you, and the kindnesses of the day extended to them will be the choicest gifts to yourself. Let your aid go beyond, "Lord help the poor." Consider yourself one of those whose commission is for this work, and make at least one home brighter and one heart thankful by your deeds outside the circle of friends and kindred.

The St. Cloud Journal, St. Cloud, Minnesota
December 24, 1868

ACKNOWLEDGMENTS

"Christmas in a Sod House" by Hugo Nisbeth, excerpted from "A Swedish Visitor of the Early Seventies," translated and edited by Roy W. Swanson, in *Minnesota History*, 8:411-7 (Dec. 1927). Used with permission.

"The Brightest Memory" from *Me* by Brenda Ueland. Copyright 1983 by the Shubert Club. Permission given courtesy of the Shubert Club, St. Paul, Minnesota.

"The Cut-Glass Christmas" from *Redbook*, December, 1980. Copyright Susan Allen Toth. Used with permission of the author.

"A Child's Christmas in Lake Wobegon" from "Winter," *Lake Wobegon Days* by Garrison Keillor. Copyright © 1985 by Garrison Keillor. All rights reserved. Reprinted with permission of Viking Penguin Inc.

"Waiting for Christmas Day" by Harrison E. Salisbury from "Victorian City in the Midwest," *Growing up in Minnesota*, edited by Chester G. Anderson, copyright University of Minnesota, Press, 1976. Used with permission.

"Christmas Eve Service at Midnight at St. Michael's" from *The Morning Glory* by Robert Bly. Copyright © 1975 by Robert Bly. Published by Harper and Row. Used with permission.

"Long Underwear and Such Things" from *From This Valley* by Clarice Olson Adelmann. Copyright 1981, Adventure Publications. Used with permission.

"A Country School Christmas" from "Letters from a Pioneer Woman" by Britania J. Livingston. Originally published in the Fairmont Daily Sentinel, June 6, 1925.

Selections by Alice L. Soffa, Arlie M. Klimes, Selma Anderson Hughes, Milton S. Johnson from *Country School Memories* edited by Bonnie Hughes Falk. Copyright 1986 Bonnie Hughes Falk. Used with permission.

"The Christmas Horses" from *On the Banks of Plum Creek* by Laura Ingalls Wilder, copyright 1937 by Laura Ingalls Wilder. Renewed by Roger L. MacBride. Published by Harper and Row. Used with permission.

Selections by Mrs. C.A. Smith, Mrs. Robert Anderson, Charles M. Loring, Mrs. W.L. Neimann from *Old Rail Fence Corners* edited by Lucy Leavenworth Wilder Morris. Published 1914. Reprinted edition 1976 by the Minnesota Historical Society Press.

Letter of Carl and Fred Bergman; Lake-of-the-Woods lumbercamp, 1913; and letter dated December 14, 1879 from *Letters from the Promised Land* edited by H. Arnold Barton. Copyright 1975 University of Minnesota Press. Pages 174, 242, 298-299. Used with permission.

Selections by Father Louis Hennepin from *Description of Louisiana*. First edition 1682, Paris, Louis XIV dedication. English edition 1698, London, second issue, William III, Prince of Orange, dedication. New translation Marion E. Cross, University of Minnesota Press, 1938.